Long-range Planning Practices
in
45 Industrial Companies

Long-range Planning Practices in 45 Industrial Companies

HAROLD W. HENRY

Associate Professor of Industrial Management
The University of Tennessee

PRENTICE-HALL, INC. *Englewood Cliffs, N.J.*

PRENTICE-HALL, INC.

ENGLEWOOD CLIFFS, N.J.

LIBRARY OF CONGRESS
CATALOG CARD NUMBER: 67-23708

PRINTED IN THE UNITED STATES OF AMERICA

B&P

To My Parents
Mr. and Mrs. Oscar Pleas Henry

With gratitude for their example of diligent work and steadfast character.

About the Author

Harold W. Henry has twelve years of experience in administrative and industrial research positions. He served as Business and Safety Coordinator for the Phoenix Memorial Laboratory and Ford Nuclear Reactor Facility at The University of Michigan, and conducted research at the Oak Ridge plants of Union Carbide Corporation. He worked as an experimental physicist and radiation safety specialist, and is a Certified Health Physicist. His earliest experience was with the Aluminum Company of America.

Dr. Henry, who is Associate Professor of Industrial Management at the University of Tennessee, earned a Ph.D. degree in business administration from the University of Michigan, where he majored in management, finance, and business economics. He holds an M.S. degree in industrial management from the University of Tennessee and a B.S. degree in physics from Maryville College (Tenn.). He formerly taught at the University of Michigan and at Eastern Michigan University.

Articles by Dr. Henry have been published in *Management of Personnel Quarterly* and *Tennessee Survey of Business*, and he has consulting experience with the National Aeronautics and Space Administration, Midland-Ross Corporation, and Union Carbide Corporation.

Why This Book Was Written

Long-range planning by managers of business corporations typically pertains to a time period beyond the current accounting year and one which extends five years into the future. In a broader sense, long-range planning means "forward" planning of a firm's activities from the present into the future as far as it is practical to plan.

Every business firm does long-range planning of a sort, but in most companies, such efforts are rather informal. This "informal" long-range planning is usually done verbally by top executives at irregular time intervals and is characterized by a lack of systematic planning procedures. It is often motivated by sagging profits, physical plant limitations, or bold action by a competitor.

Since the mid-1950's, and especially since 1960, a growing number of firms have recognized that this type of expedient planning is often inefficient and ineffective. These firms have developed more formal approaches to long-range planning which usually include specific planning procedures and time schedules, clear assignments of planning responsibility, and the development of written divisional and corporation long-range plans.

A rapidly increasing body of literature in the last few years has focused on many aspects of long-range corporate planning, but much of it has provided little practical guidance for the business manager who wanted to "formalize" his planning activities. In this book, I have reviewed and analyzed to varying degrees the long-range planning systems in 45 corporations, including some of the largest and most successful business firms in the United States. Most of these companies are among those who formalized their planning activities in the last few years. Therefore, the focus of the book is on "formal" long-range corporate planning practices. Primary emphasis is given to the organization and the administrative procedures for planning in industrial companies.

In chapter 1, reasons for following more systematic long-range planning procedures are reviewed, and some of the major variables which influenced the approaches to planning in the companies studied are discussed.

In chapters 2 and 3, the planning practices which were found in 45 industrial firms are reported and analyzed. These practices pertain to responsibility assignments for planning, economic and market forecasting, corporate objectives and strategies, administrative procedures for developing plans, the nature of long-range plans, computer utilization in planning, and company evaluations of formalized planning.

In chapters 4, 5, and 6, the long-range planning systems in International Minerals and Chemical Corporation, Motorola Inc., and a major automobile company are reviewed. These case reports illustrate significantly different, but effective, approaches to long-range planning.

In chapter 7, the evolution of planning systems and current trends in long-range planning are discussed, and a summary appraisal is made of formalized long-range corporate planning.

Many examples of specific planning procedures are included in this book, and they were selected to illustrate sound long-range planning. No attempt is made to outline a single best system, because different approaches can be effective. Thus, the book is intended to serve as a general guide for the corporate executive, operating manager, or staff specialist. It should also provide valuable insight into the processes of business management and decision-making in large corporations for the student of business administration.

The corporations which provided data for this book are distributed among ten major industries as follows: chemical–six, container–two, electrical and electronic equipment–seven, farm and construction machinery–four, food–four, motor vehicle–five, petroleum–six, pharmaceutical–three, rubber–three, and steel–five. Of these companies 25 are among the 50 largest firms in the United States, based on annual sales, and 40 of them are included in the top 160 firms. Their combined annual sales account for approximately 15 per cent of the Gross National Product in the United States.

I personally interviewed executives or planning specialists in over half of the companies investigated, and these persons provided a major portion of the data for this book. Their essential contribution is gratefully acknowledged. A few of these individuals who made significant contributions can be named, while others who deserve much credit asked to remain anonymous.

John T. Hickey, Vice President, Planning, in Motorola Inc., was very cooperative in providing the data on long-range planning in his company which are reviewed in chapter 5.

The long-range planning system at International Minerals and Chemical Corporation (chapter 4) was described carefully by Donald J. Smalter,

Director of Strategic Planning, Dr. Sidney Singer, Manager of the Management Sciences Section, and Robert A. Mocella, Corporate Planner.

Clayton F. Ruebensaal, Director of Corporate Planning, Uniroyal—United States Rubber Company, made available the "Function Analysis" for his position (Table 2) and discussed the planning system in his company.

Professor Franklin G. Moore and Professor George S. Odiorne, of the University of Michigan Graduate School of Business Administration, made many constructive comments in reviewing the initial manuscript of this book.

I wish to extend my thanks to each of these persons and to all other executives, planners, educators, and management consultants who discussed corporate long-range planning orally or in correspondence.

Finally, my wife, Zurma, deserves much credit for her support and cooperation during all of the stages of developing this book, and for her efforts in typing the final manuscript.

Harold Wilkinson Henry

Contents

Chapter Page

List of Tables

Long-range Planning Practices

in

45 Industrial Companies

Chapter 1

The Development and Variability of Formalized Planning Systems

Long-range planning is the process of deciding what to do in an uncommitted future time period to achieve certain goals. When complete, such planning should provide answers to the basic questions—Who? What? When? Where? Why? and How? The time period for which long-range plans are developed will vary in length with the nature of the planned activities and the degree of uncertainty about the future. For example, long-range planning of some agricultural activities is limited to a 30-day period by the available weather forecasts. At the other extreme, long-range planning for timber production, which has a long planting to harvest cycle, may extend 80 or 90 years into the future.

FORMALIZED LONG-RANGE PLANNING—AN EMERGING ESSENTIAL

The type of planning which business managers have done over the years has shifted with the situation they faced. When changes were gradual, a leisurely planning pace was apparently satisfactory. However, as changes in the business environment occurred more frequently, business planning had to be intensified.

World War II created many changes which affected business firms. One author has stated that it was "the greatest single factor contributing to the development of formalized long-range planning." [1] He cited several reasons for this belief, as follows:

1. the demand for war goods induced rapid company growth,
2. physical and human resources were scarce and needed to be used efficiently,
3. government expenditures for research and development produced many technological advances, and
4. many postwar business managers gained valuable experience in systematic, futuristic government organizations during the war period.[2]

These reasons are doubtless valid, but other factors have contributed to the increased emphasis on systematic long-range planning more recently.

First, business firms have continued to grow rapidly in size. Expansion has resulted from a desire to satisfy the increasing demands of a growing and more affluent domestic population. Economic activity has been at a high level for several years, so that business operations have been profitable and the climate for growth has been favorable. New foreign markets have developed because political barriers to free international trade have been removed, underdeveloped countries have started to industrialize, and developed countries have attained greater purchasing power. Therefore, this rapid growth of industrial firms has required extensive forward planning of production facilities and marketing programs in order to provide goods of proper quantity and quality whenever and wherever demanded.

Secondly, business management has become very complex in recent years. Production processes and equipment have become more complicated and expensive as automation has spread to many types of manufacturing. Product lines of most firms have become more diversified and the amount of variation in a given product line has increased greatly. In addition, the geographical dispersion of raw material inputs, production facilities, and markets has increased significantly. Thus, these developments have also intensified the need for more systematic long-range planning.

Thirdly, the level of expenditure for research and development by industrial firms and government agencies has increased at a phenomenal rate, and the resulting technological changes and new products have exceeded all expectations. The primary reason for the upward-spiraling level of corporation spending for research has been the intense competition between firms to develop new or improved products, and even complacent firms have been forced to join the race when their profits declined. As product life cycles have been shortened because of rapid innovation, higher investments in new facilities and more expensive marketing activities have been required. Thus, poor decisions have become much more costly, and the process of "creative destruction" [3] has taken its toll. Therefore, corporation executives have been forced to consider most carefully the future impact of current decisions, and this has demanded more systematic methods for making decisions.

A fourth reason for the growing interest in formalized long-range planning has been the need to ration limited funds amongst an increasing number of investment opportunities. Even the very largest firms can no longer invest in every "good" opportunity, but must analyze carefully each competing proposal in order to make the best decision. Also, the level of capital spending by business firms in a given year represents a sizable fraction of their total net worth, and careless use of financial assets could cause serious losses. In the past few years the magnitude of total spending each year for new plants and equipment has been approximately 7 per cent of the annual Gross National Product in the United States. Thus, more systematic methods for investigating and evaluating capital spending proposals have become necessary in order to insure continuing economic health for business firms and the nation.

Finally, the manner of spending by the federal government has forced the manufacturers of goods for defense and other uses to plan more systematically. Such planning has permitted them to anticipate changes in demand sooner and to become more flexible. Thus, firms in the aerospace-electronics industry which were major government suppliers made some of the earliest and most significant developments in long-range planning.

VARIABLES IN COMPANY APPROACHES TO LONG-RANGE PLANNING

In the 45 corporations studied, approaches to long-range planning varied widely. Some companies had highly formalized planning systems, many had formalized planning to a degree, and a few firms planned for the future in a very informal manner. The planning approach in each company had undoubtedly been influenced by the personalities of past and present executives, company tradition, the nature of the industry, and other factors. However, four variables were detected during the study which seemed to have a significant influence on the manner in which current long-range planning was carried out. They were: (1) the philosophy and leadership of top executives, (2) the orientation of a company to change, (3) the organization for long-range planning, and (4) the activity focus of forward planning. Each of these variables will be discussed in terms of its impact on long-range planning effectiveness.

PHILOSOPHY AND LEADERSHIP OF TOP EXECUTIVES

The success of long-range planning efforts in each business corporation seemed to be related directly to the extent of active interest and leadership of the President and other top executives. This belief was explicit or implicit in statements made by a significant number of corporation representatives. A typical comment was as follows: "One of the leading features of our arrangement is the enthusiastic active support given to long-range planning by the President; this, in our opinion, is a must for it to be effective. . . ." Another person stated: "It is obvious that a long-range planning function can be effective only if the Chief Executive Officer is interested in it and willing to give it considerable support."

Lack of active involvement by the firm's top executive was mentioned by one staff specialist as a limitation to planning effectiveness. In another company, the Vice President—Corporate Development—said that a staff planner in his firm had to work with one executive and the members of his division for three months "prodding" them to develop plans. Thus, the clear implication was that the indifference of this executive led to ineffective long-range planning.

Recently, the President of one large corporation exhibited positive leadership in formalizing long-range planning in his company by requesting written long-range plans from each division. His instructions, in a memorandum to Division Vice Presidents and General Managers, reflected a sound managerial philosophy of planning and outlined several important types of information to be included in divisional long-range plans. This directive ended with the following justification for developing formal long-range plans:

> Carefully prepared divisional long range plans are essential if group and corporate management are to evaluate properly the many demands for research and capital funds. Moreover, the thought process necessary in preparing a long-range plan, the material developed, and the timing of submission should prove helpful to your normal sales, income and capital budgeting effort. Finally, and most important, your plan should be valuable as a guide to you and your associates in operating your division.

A corporate planning specialist drafted a large part of the document referred to, but it was endorsed, announced, and distributed by the President. Therefore, his leadership will surely motivate others in the company to plan more thoroughly, especially if it is continuous and aggressive. This conclusion can be applied to any business firm, for the philosophy and attitude of the top executives will have a major impact on the nature and effectiveness of the firm's long-range planning system.

Company Orientation to Change

A company's orientation to change, especially technological innovation, had an important bearing on how it approached long-range planning. In general, this orientation can be one of initiation, one of reaction, one containing some degree of each, or one containing neither (status-quoism). Companies which invest heavily in technical and business research are usually the ones that initiate changes through innovations in products, processes, or management techniques. Others wait until some competitor introduces a change and then react to it by making changes to protect their interests. A few companies never innovate or change and eventually cease to exist.

Many companies take action to direct their future to some degree, but much change is adaptive in nature. This may be due to a passive orientation, or it may be due to political, social, and economic changes which cannot be significantly altered by company actions.

An illustration of a company orientation to change, which is both initiating and reactive, is found in a statement by the Chairman and President of General Motors Corporation. When a two-year, 2-billion dollar capital expenditure program was reported, they explained:

> These expenditures for plants and equipment are necessary to keep our products in the forefront of advancing technology, to keep our plant facilities modern and efficient, and to meet the demands of growing markets in the United States and abroad. The growth rate over the long term is upward, and GM must be ready with the right products in the right quantities at the right time.[4]

Most of the companies investigated had a similar outlook, but not all had been successful in the past in planning the scope, timing, scale, and nature of future activities so as to achieve the desired results. For example, the Manager of Development for one division of a major chemical corporation told how the approval for building a new production plant was delayed unnecessarily until demand exceeded output capacity, with a resulting loss of sales and customers.

A company's orientation to change may be a reflection of the philosophy of its top executives, but it is usually developed over a long period of time and may not reflect fully the desire of the present executives. A company which expects and plans for change is most likely to be successful, but this orientation alone will not insure effective planning. The methods used to develop and implement plans for the future can be the critical factor for success in achieving objectives.

ORGANIZATION FOR PLANNING

In companies which were engaged in systematic long-range planning, specific planning activities were assigned to persons at various positions in the firm's organization structure. This organizational arrangement for long-range planning differed in many ways among the companies investigated. However, one pattern was most common and was being adopted by more firms each year. The typical arrangement consisted of a corporate staff group (or individual) that coordinated planning and analyzed potential new ventures, while the managers of major operating (or line) units were responsible for developing long-range plans for their respective departments or divisions. Final authority for approving long-range plans usually resided either with the President, a committee of top executives, or the Board of Directors.

The emphasis was typically on divisional planning, because most of the companies were organized into major operating units on the basis of product groups or geographical location. In this type of structure, the divisions were integrated and self-sufficient to a high degree, and they were usually designated as profit centers. Therefore, planning could be largely independent and complete for such units, and each division manager could be held responsible for current profit performance and for planning future activities. In companies that were highly decentralized, such managers were assigned a fraction of the company's resources—money, equipment, and other assets—and they were expected to use these resources in a profitable manner on a continuing basis into the future.

Even though long-range planning was generally assigned to major operating units, no divisions were completely independent, and the investigation revealed an increasing emphasis on integrated corporate planning. The corporate planning staffs in the companies which had formalized long-range planning did not merely put a common binder on divisional plans or summarize divisional financial projections to form a corporate plan. They often reviewed divisional plans and pointed out areas of conflict, inconsistencies, deficiencies, areas of low profitability, or attractive new investment opportunities. By this action, an integrated plan was sought which would maximize the benefits to the corporation as a whole.

Holding companies, such as some large petroleum corporations, no longer served merely as central bankers for their subsidiaries, for they too had established corporate planning staffs to analyze, integrate, and coordinate the activities of their sub-units.

Any change in the basic organization structure of a company affected the approach to long-range planning. At least three of the 45 companies which were studied had reorganized in recent years. They had centralized authority to a significant degree in order to cut costs, integrate functions, and provide better control. Thus, the change in the basic organization structure in each of these firms had given a more important role to its corporation planning function.

The organization for long-range planning was also related to the nature of a firm's product line. Some industrial companies produced one major type of product and, even though large in size, they engaged in activities which were necessarily highly integrated. These companies were commonly organized on a functional basis. Therefore, corporate planning was highly centralized, because any single operating unit was usually not self-sufficient enough to make independent plans. Some steel, oil, and automobile manufacturing companies followed this pattern.

In such companies, the corporate planning staff had a more dominant role in long-range planning than line managers. A Vice President in one steel corporation stated that "operating managers are not responsible for long-range planning, but their job is to make money on current operations." This philosophy seemed to follow the old recipe of separating planning from doing, but this executive added that "line managers think about ways to make money in the future and submit many ideas to the corporate planning staff."

This centralized, or "top-down" approach to long-range planning was evident to a high degree in only a few of the companies studied. On the other hand, the decentralized or "bottom-up" approach was not absolute in any of the companies, even though divisions in a few firms were highly autonomous within certain policy and financial restraints imposed by the corporation. The typical approach could be called "integrated upward and downward planning." In such systems, the divisions sought to project or extend current operations, while corporate planners sought to integrate divisional plans and to extend company activities in areas where no single division was responsible. This latter pattern of organizing should lead to more effective long-range planning than when a company is highly centralized or highly decentralized.

ACTIVITY FOCUS OF PLANNING

The approach to long-range planning also varied in terms of the primary activity focus of the planning efforts. In some companies, financial planning, with projected income statements for five years, was the major thrust. In others, capital spending proposals and the expansion or improvement of facilities was the primary planning activity.

In some firms, new product development, market development, or marketing planning received the most attention.

In a few corporations, growth and expansion by merger or acquisition was a continuing focal point of planning. In other firms, this was an infrequent planning activity.

All of these functional activities were important, but when efforts were concentrated on certain ones, the approach to long-range planning was unbalanced. However, a majority of the companies which had formal planning assignments had developed an integrated planning system to give proper attention to all of these aspects of long-range planning. This type of balanced activity focus should be sought to achieve the most effective long-range planning.

OTHER VARIABLES IN PLANNING APPROACHES

The focus of long-range planning in the companies studied was not on some remote future time period, as the term "long-range" implies. Instead, it was on "forward" planning from the present into the distant future, with a decreasing amount of detailed planning as more faraway periods were considered.

A finite period of time ranging from three to 20 years was the span of written plans and forecasts in these companies. A period of five years was most common, even though it was recognized that current decisions can have a significant impact on future activities and earnings for much longer periods of time.

A distinction was often made between "strategic" and "operational" planning. The former considered the broad approach or general plans to achieve certain longer-term objectives, while operational planning involved more detailed, specific aspects of implementing strategic plans or extending current activities.

Summary

The approach to long-range planning varied in many respects in the firms studied. Each company wished to continue as a profitable entity, but the philosophies and methodologies of management differed significantly. Each firm also recognized the changing nature of the business environment and the importance of long-range planning. The emerging pattern of management was to develop more formal administrative procedures, methods of communication, and information-handling systems. In this way, strategic forward planning to cope with this change and to help create it was more effective.

Footnotes for Chapter 1

[1] Brian W. Scott, *Long-Range Planning in American Industry* (New York: American Management Association, Inc., 1965), p. 52.

[2] *Ibid.*, pp. 52–55.

[3] "Creative destruction" means that a product or process is made obsolete or "destroyed" by an innovation of a competitor in a free-enterprise economic system, yet society is benefited. This concept was introduced and explained by Joseph A. Schumpeter in *Capitalism, Socialism, and Democracy* (3rd ed.; New York: Harper & Brothers, Publishers, 1950), pp. 81–86.

[4] Frederic G. Donner and John F. Gordon, *General Motors Annual Report—1964* (New York: General Motors Corporation, 1965), p. 2.

Chapter 2

Planning Practices—Organizing, Forecasting, Goal and Strategy Formulation

Since corporate planning is done by people who are employed by business firms, a review of specific responsibility assignments in major industrial companies should provide a clearer image of the process of long-range planning. Therefore, the assignments for individuals and groups in the firms which were studied are reported and discussed in the first part of this chapter.

RESPONSIBILITY ASSIGNMENTS FOR LONG-RANGE PLANNING

Planning Responsibilities of Top Executives

Long-range planning activities were formalized to some extent in 38 of the 45 companies which were studied. In the other seven firms, planning for the future was done informally at the top executive level. The focal point for the formalized planning activities was at a high staff level in the corporation executive offices. Either a staff officer or a highly-placed staff specialist was assigned an important role in long-range planning in these firms, as indicated in Table I.

TABLE 1

RESPONSIBILITY ASSIGNMENTS FOR LONG-RANGE PLANNING IN 45 COMPANIES

Major Planning Responsibility Assigned to:	*Companies No.*
Vice President—Planning (or equivalent title)	16
Executive Vice President or Group Vice President	3
Vice President—Finance or Controller	6
Director of Forward Planning who reported to the Chairman of the Board of Directors	1
Director of Planning (or equivalent title) who reported to the President	5
Vice President (limited planning functions)	3
Specific Planning Units (responsible executive undetermined)	4
Companies Having Formal Planning Assignments	38
Companies Having No Formal Planning	7
All Companies Studied	45

Note: In 22 of these companies, a committee of top executives had important long-range planning responsibilities. In 26 companies, planning assignments were made to staff personnel in operating units, in addition to corporate staff assignments.

In 16 of the companies, responsibility for planning activities was assigned to a Vice President whose title included either plans, planning, corporate planning, long-range planning and new product development, planning and control, marketing and corporate planning, research and planning, corporate planning and development, development, corporate development, business development, or organization. Corporate staff planning groups reported to the planning executive in each of these companies, and one member of such staffs usually served as the key long-range planning coordinator for the corporation.

To indicate the nature of the duties of these executives, the major functions of the Vice President—Corporate Planning—in one firm are outlined herein. These assignments, as condensed from this executive's formal job description, were to:

1. formulate corporate objectives and policies (for approval of the President),
2. develop action programs (for approval of the President),
3. direct the planning staff in activities of market research, economic and business analysis, and planning for products, facilities, and acquisitions,
4. evaluate market growth potential,
5. initiate and coordinate overall marketing strategy,
6. coordinate and integrate divisional planning activities,
7. direct and participate in a search for opportunities for business growth and development,
8. evaluate possible mergers or acquisitions and negotiate desired ones,
9. direct the corporate handling of proposed new processes and products,
10. develop priorities for major new products and projects, recommend special research projects to the President, and audit the progress of projects,
11. provide an information service to other executives,
12. review major capital expenditures in relation to corporate objectives, and
13. recommend short-term and long-term budgets.

The scope of this executive's functions was broader than that of the typical planning executive and reflected a more centralized approach to planning than many firms followed, but this list includes most of the functions that were assigned to any planning executive in the companies which were investigated.

In several other companies, executives which were not designated as planning officers had important planning assignments. In three companies, an Executive Vice President or Group Vice President was responsible for long-range planning. In six other firms, the Vice President-Finance or the Controller was responsible for coordinating the planning efforts. Vice Presidents for Commercial Development, Steel Manufacturing and Research, and Acquisitions, respectively, had limited planning responsibilities in three additional companies. Thus, more than half of the 45 companies had assigned key planning functions to a corporate officer.

In a majority of the companies which had formalized long-range planning, a Director of Planning, or a position with a similar title, was also designated. These planning "Directors" generally reported to a Vice President, but in one company, the person in this position reported to the Chairman of the Board of Directors. In five other firms, persons in similar positions served on the President's personal staff. In a few of the companies, the Director of Planning was assigned at the second level below that of a Vice President.

In spite of the high degree of staff participation in long-range planning (and domination in a few firms), most staff planners and executives considered planning to be a basic responsibility of operating managers and top executives. One Director of Corporate Development summarized this view in these words:

> The "prime" responsibility of planning in any corporation in the final analysis rests with the Chief Executive Officer, usually the President. Under him the divisions, division planners, and the (corporate) staff departments all assist in making and carrying out long-range plans based on company objectives.

Another Director of Corporate Planning stated that "the President is the only corporate planner and the Corporate Planning Department serves as a tool for use by the President."

Thus, top executives were fully responsible for long-range planning, as for other managerial functions, but the scope of planning assignments and the personal attention devoted to planning varied widely among executives in different companies.

Functions of Corporate Planning Staffs

As indicated previously, the role of corporate planning staffs was generally viewed as that of performing specialized functions to help the busy executive or operating manager, and to act as his "long-range conscience."

William F. May, Chairman of the Board of Directors of American Can Company, has defined two major endeavors of a corporate planning staff as follows:

> Corporate planning and development has a double function: first, to guide and assist the divisions in the formulation of their business plans; second, to develop an overall corporate business plan that will comprise both the sum of the divisional plans and the growth objectives of the corporation as a whole.[1]

This statement summarizes the views of many of the staff planning specialists who were interviewed about their jobs.

To illustrate specific assignments of corporate planning staffs, the duties of the Corporate Business Planning unit in one company are listed as follows:

1. develop forms and procedures for use in preparing divisional long-range business plans,

2. prepare and issue planning instructions and schedules to each operating unit,
3. obtain accounting data, financial definitions, and market research data for use by operating units (divisions) in preparing long-range plans,
4. schedule review meetings during the planning period with divisional planners and managers, and suggest those who should attend to the operating units,
5. receive business plans from each operating unit and consolidate them into a corporate plan,
6. review the consolidated plan in detail and prepare a written report which includes a broad corporate analysis, a critique, and recommendations for revisions,
7. discuss proposed changes with operating groups and resolve conflicts by consulting with operating units and other staff groups *continually* during the planning cycle, and
8. present revised consolidated plans to the Executive Committee for review and approval.

During this sequence of activities by the corporate planning staff, the corporate financial staff consolidated budgets which were prepared by the operating units to correspond to their business plans. The business plan and the financial plan (budgets) were reviewed and coordinated by the planning and financial staffs before presentation to the Executive Committee for final approval.

The preceding list of functions stressed the coordinating and integrating role of a corporate planning staff in preparing a business plan. In the Uniroyal—United States Rubber Company, the Director of Corporate Planning fulfilled a "forward planning" research and analysis role in addition to the common coordinating role. The duties of this key staff planner, as described in the company's "Function Analysis" manual, are reproduced in Table 2.

TABLE 2

DUTIES OF THE DIRECTOR OF CORPORATE PLANNING
UNIROYAL—UNITED STATES RUBBER COMPANY

1. *Consults, advises* and *recommends* (with the Corporate Planning Committee) on the formulation of corporate goals, objectives and strategy with reference to the types of business and fields of endeavor the Company will pursue.
2. *Develops* techniques to be used in broad Company-wide forward planning and in specific Five-Year Forward Growth and Profit Improvement (GAPI) Programs of the Divisions.
3. *Counsels* and *advises* the Operating Divisions (through their respective Com-

mercial Development Managers) and pertinent Corporate staff personnel concerning planning methodology and the development of forward planning programs.

4. *Conducts* preliminary reviews of the Divisional GAPI Program presentations with the Divisional staffs, the Director of Economic Analysis and Corporate Planning and his staff and makes recommendations to Divisional management, the Corporate Planning Committee, and the President concerning gaps between Divisional capabilities and corporate goals.
5. *Prepares* minutes and *maintains* follow-up of all Divisional GAPI Program presentations and status reviews for the President and the Corporate Planning Committee.
6. *Consolidates* the capital requirements emanating from the Divisional GAPI Programs and assists in determining the priority of employing capital within the limits set by the financial officers of the Company.
7. *Conducts* continued surveillance of technological, economic and world political environments to ascertain changes affecting the survival and growth of the Company.
8. *Participates* actively in major divisional and corporate research and development meetings, and marketing and planning seminars.
9. *Conducts* continued research into the broad industrial and consumer marketing areas in which the Company is currently operating, or in which the Company's potential would enable it to function profitably, to determine the various alternative directions for insuring growth and profit maximization.
10. *Conducts* continued study of the potential effects on Corporate growth and profits of acquisition, integration and divestment possibilities, by screening or adding to prospects developed at the divisional level, and utilizes the financial services of the acquisition section of the Economic Analysis and Corporate Planning Department in finalizing decisions on selected opportunities.

The functional assignments of corporate planning staffs were quite different in scope among the companies studied. For example, market research and economic analysis were performed by the planning staff or by a unit located adjacent to it in some firms. In others, these functions were performed by a group which was widely separated from the planning staff in the organization structure. However, in this latter case, close liaison existed between the groups. In some companies, a function of the planning staff was to prepare a written analysis of the future business environment which was based on forecasts made by the economists.

One Director of Corporate Planning performed an unusual task when his company recently formalized long-range planning. He structured and wrote a five-year plan to serve as an example for operating units when developing their own plans. This sample plan was realistic, for it was based on interviews with the manager of one division of the corporation, and was reviewed and revised by this operating manager.

Planning staffs served sometimes as a research group for a top executive, and spent most of their efforts on special projects in which he had a current interest.

In one highly decentralized company in which long-range financial planning was coordinated by the Controller's staff, a new group called the Corporate Planning Operation was established in 1964. The Director of the group reported to the President. The assignments of this staff unit were to handle acquisitions, to study potential new markets, and to develop procedures to more effectively integrate decentralized sales efforts throughout the corporation. This group was formed to satisfy emerging needs in the company, and these assignments illustrate the diverse nature of formal planning functions.

Some corporate planning staffs monitored the performance of operating units periodically by comparing results to plans, and some analyzed the performance of major competitors. Planning units also made investment analyses, and one planner reported that his group assisted the Executive Committee in preparing divisional planning guidelines which included rate-of-return and profit goals and capital investment limitations. Another planning specialist said that his group developed criteria and provided information for strategic decision-making by top management.

A Vice President in one steel corporation stated that his long-range planning group was the catalyst for planning in the company. He said they pushed things from the top such as new product or process development, served as project leaders on task forces, and followed through on the implementation of plans. They also analyzed capital expenditure proposals, served as his "eyes and ears," and developed 20-year plans. These activities indicated a centralized planning role for the corporate planning unit in this firm, with less emphasis on coordination.

This type of dominant staff planning was found in only a few of the companies which were investigated. These firms had highly integrated activities and/or functional organization structures. A Vice President in another steel company expressed the philosophy of centralized planning in these words: "The job of planners is to have the corporation where it should be in future years, after top management sets the goal."

Planning Responsibilities of Divisional Planners and Committees

Divisional planning staffs or coordinators existed in at least 26 of the companies which had corporate planning staffs, and this group or person usually reported to the general manager of a particular division. The planning units which were found in company divisions included part-time coordinators, small staffs, and special committees. In some companies, divisional planning assignments did not exist because the division managers utilized other functional staffs for planning, or because all planning was centralized in the corporation offices.

Divisional planners were primarily responsible for:

1. obtaining and assembling information to include in divisional long-range plans,
2. discussing various aspects of the plan with operating managers,
3. coordinating all planning activities in the division, and
4. cooperating with the corporate planning staff and following its guidance.

Their assignments were generally not as broad in scope as those of corporate planners. However, the functions were similar in some large companies, especially if the divisions were large and relatively independent. Some divisional planners had extensive experience in their jobs and, in a few cases, felt that they were doing the bulk of the planning in the company. One such person said of his planning counterparts at the corporation level, "They're learning!"

One company had committees in different divisions which were each concerned with a particular commodity line, and they met bimonthly as continuing planning groups. These committees were distinct from the Commercial Development or Market Research groups which coordinated the preparation of divisional five-year plans, and they were called SPED Boards. Their name was derived from the membership—representatives of Sales, Production, Engineering, and Development. Each committee revised regularly the previous estimates of sales, prices, costs, and other variables, and their data were used in developing and revising five-year plans. Several of these groups existed in each division, and they performed a very useful planning function.

PLANNING RESPONSIBILITIES OF CONTROLLERS' STAFFS

The corporate planning coordinators who served on a controller's staff performed many of the same functions which were done by corporate planning staffs. They developed forms and instructions for use in all operating units, reviewed and consolidated long-range plans, and monitored performance. Their focus was on financial planning and control, but some planning systems with this orientation were highly developed and fairly broad in scope. A case study of a system of this type in a major automobile company is contained in chapter 6.

The corporate planning functions in companies where the controller was responsible were generally not as broad in scope as those assigned to separate planning groups. Also, they did not have the "forward planning" emphasis of seeking and analyzing new products, processes, or ventures. They were primarily concerned with:

1. rate-of-return analyses of proposed capital investments, and
2. profit analyses of long-range plans which operating units had developed.

In some companies, internal struggles over the assignment of planning functions had taken place between proponents of a separate planning staff and proponents of the existing controller's organization. The Manager of Planning Coordination in a company where the "separate planner" forces had won this battle believed that a controller's staff was severely limited in performing planning assignments. He said that "accountants think only backwards," in reference to their traditional role of historical reporting, "and can never be effective in a long-range planning function." This may be true in many situations, but much depends on the capabilities of the individuals involved.

Financial planning is certainly an essential element of effective long-range planning. However, planning for the future should be much broader in scope than the functions which a controller's staff are usually trained to perform. For this reason, the best organizational arrangement for formalized long-range planning seems to be to provide a separate planning staff at the corporate level and also in each major operating unit of a company. However, the financial staff can perform important analytical assignments in such a long-range planning system.

COMPOSITE SUMMARY OF STAFF PLANNING FUNCTIONS

Many different words were used by executives and planning specialists to describe the functions of corporate planning staffs. A composite summary of the functions performed by such planners would include analyzing, interpreting, educating, cajoling, and forcing. Corporate planners also served as researchers, forecasters, developers and communicators of instructions and ideas, catalysts, integrators and reviewers of plans, consultants, monitors, and policemen. They filled important roles as dreamers, initiators, planning system engineers, and administrators.

The major emphasis in decentralized companies was that a corporate planning group existed to help the divisions. In these companies, the words advising, consulting, assisting, and coordinating were commonly used to describe the functions of the corporate planning staff. In fact, this role was the most prevalent one among the companies studied. However, a spectrum of roles emerged in which the corporate planning groups in different companies exhibited various degrees of domination of the planning function. One end point on this spectrum was represented by a steel corporation whose

Vice President stated, "Long-range planning in this company is top-side; it is like an umbrella."

The size of corporate planning staffs and the scope of their assigned responsibilities varied widely among the companies which were investigated. In Motorola Inc., an advisory and coordinating role was assigned to a single planning specialist who became Vice President, Planning, in 1965. At the other extreme, the 80-member Planning and Development Division of International Minerals and Chemical Corporation was responsible for strategic planning, market research, venture development, information processing, operations research, and organizational planning. However, the typical corporate planning staff had two to six members and served primarily to coordinate long-range planning by the operating units.

Assignment and Selection Policies for Staff Planners

One Director of Corporate Planning said that "a person shouldn't be in planning too long." This view was a common one, for several companies reported that persons were not assigned permanently to staff planning groups. One firm had adopted a general company policy of rotating all staff and operating people. Another firm assigned an employee to the corporate long-range planning staff for about two years, then to a similar position in one division for one or two years, and finally to an operating unit. In a third company, employees of the Corporate Planning Department worked on staff studies in one or more divisions for about five years, and then many of them moved into management jobs in other departments.

The desired qualifications of a person for a planning assignment were generally very high. One Vice President said that "a planning coordinator should be a person qualified to be a good operating manager." Another executive stated that a successful planner should have a good measure of creativity, be a keen analyst, and be effective in working with others.

In one company which utilized task forces for long-range planning activities, highly qualified persons were sought for such assignments in various divisions. Basic company policy dictated that individuals should be made available as needed, for such assignments were considered very important.

The need for a considerable amount of accounting and control skill was reported by one executive, because his firm had experienced a deficiency in this skill among some members of its planning staff.

Appraisal of the Role of Staff Planners

One Director of Corporate Planning believed that planning should be an integral part of the job of top managers instead of a separate staff function. He expressed his management philosophy in these words:

> Planning is too important to have a planner (middle manager) tinkering with it. Planners are trying to develop the planning mystique, but in a really well-run company, you don't need a corporate planner (as in General Motors).

This planner viewed his job as that of a "system entrepreneur," and his stated goal was "to work myself and all division planners out of a job."

Most other planning specialists who were interviewed would probably disagree sharply with this view. However, other persons also mentioned the danger of the "planning cult" and the belief that many corporate planners had an improper conception of their role. One Vice President reported that some planners in his company felt possessive toward long-range plans when formal planning was first introduced. He added that this attitude was one factor which reduced the effectiveness of the planning efforts.

The planner previously quoted who wanted to eliminate his function believed that "there is also one best way to plan—a logical sequence to follow." He said:

> In the next ten to 20 years, a highly systematized method of planning will be used by all companies. The present quibbling over methods will be forgotten. In time, the controller's office should be able to do the bookkeeping and top management should do the strategic planning.

Whether this forecast comes true or not, it does indicate a trend which seems clear. Planning is becoming more systematic and more formalized in many companies. Staff planners are increasing rapidly in number, their functions are expanding in scope, and their influence on the future performance of business firms seems to be significant. At the same time, top executives and division managers are also giving more time and effort to planning.

The justification for staff planners is the same as for any other staff function. Top managers have a limited amount of time, energy, and specialized capability. Business management is becoming more complex and the amount of resources utilized by a company in total and for individual projects is growing larger. The timing of actions is also becoming more critical, techniques are being used which require specialized training, competition is more intense, and the consequences of mistakes are more severe. Thus, staff planners can perform valuable services for a business corporation, if their function is viewed as one of specialized assistance to the managers who are responsible for utilizing the company's resources in a profitable manner.

Summary—Organizing for Long-Range Planning

After analyzing many different long-range planning systems, there does not seem to be a single ideal system which would have universal application.

Significantly different approaches to such planning can be effective, as illustrated by the case studies in chapters 4, 5, and 6. The ability and efforts of the responsible individuals are primary determinants of long-range planning success, but clear-cut planning assignments and systematic planning procedures are also essential for maximum planning efficiency and effectiveness.

The organization for long-range planning should be tailored to fit each individual business firm. When designing such a system, one should consider the management philosophy of the company's top executives, the size and geographical distribution of the firm's activities, the nature of the product lines and functional activities of the company, the existing and ideal organization structures, and the capabilities of available personnel to fill planning assignments.

ROLE OF ECONOMIC AND MARKET FORECASTING IN PLANNING

In planning the future activities of a business firm, one of the most fundamental tasks is to predict the nature of the business environment in the coming years. The social, political, economic, and technological changes which will occur in future years should be anticipated as accurately and as soon as possible. Otherwise, long-range planning may be built on a crumbling foundation. Changes in the environment will be translated into certain levels of demand for various types of products in each future time period. Therefore, a business firm needs to forecast the demand for the products it plans to manufacture and market. To understand more clearly how forecasts are made and utilized in long-range planning, the practices of selected companies are reviewed below.

SOURCES OF ECONOMIC FORECASTS

Full-time economists were employed for short-range and long-range forecasting by many of the companies which were investigated, but others depended entirely on the services of private economists. Some firms utilized forecasts from both sources, and a few companies made little use of either.

Among the ten industries represented, the petroleum companies generally employed the largest number of economists—up to 20 on some corporate staffs. Individual economists were assigned to specialized areas of forecasting. For example, in one petroleum company, some economists concentrated on the general domestic economy, others focused on the international economy, and still others viewed the economic outlook for the petroleum industry.

PRODUCT DEMAND FORECASTING PROCEDURES

The typical pattern of demand forecasting included three steps. First, the general economic environment for the next five to ten years was appraised. Next, the total demand for each product of an entire industry was forecast. Finally, sales forecasts were made for each product which a given company expected to market. These different phases of forecasting were often assigned to different groups in a particular company. The sales forecasts were generally made by a market research, commercial research, or marketing services staff.

To illustrate this general pattern of forecasting, the procedure followed in one large international petroleum company will be reviewed.

First, forecasts of economic conditions for the next seven years were obtained from affiliates around the world and from corporation economists. These data were assembled by the corporate General Economics Department into a "yellow book" on "the economics of the world as the company sees it."

This information was then sent to the Coordination and Planning Department, where economic variables were translated into petroleum variables and published in a "green book." Included were many types of statistical data, such as the demand for each product in each market area for each type of buyer. For example, the total demand in each market area for automobile fuel, jet fuel, kerosene, and other products was estimated for each of the next seven years.

In the third step, the Marketing Department forecasted the company's share of the total demand for each product in each market in a "red book." These data then provided a basis for long-range facility planning and for preparing capital investment proposals.

In a major steel corporation, a different procedure was followed for estimating future product demand to serve as a guide in developing five-year plans. First, the population size and growth trends in each of several market areas were determined. Next, the consumption of each steel-using product in each market area was estimated, using projections of the level of general economic activity for future years which were provided by outside consultants. Finally, the steel demand was calculated for each product in each market by multiplying the weight of the steel required for one product by the estimated number of units of the product to be sold.

This technique provided a total demand forecast for steel for the next five years which served as the basis for long-range operational planning. Top management set a goal for the company of X per cent of total industry sales, and the ingot tonnage requirements to meet this goal were calculated for each product in each sales district. The procedure for developing and approving long-range plans in this company will be reviewed in chapter 3.

Economic and Market Data for Use in Forward Planning

The corporate planning staff in many companies included a brief set of "Economic Assumptions" in the instruction manuals which they provided to all divisions for guidance in developing long-range plans. A few companies permitted divisions to use their own economic forecasts as a basis for planning, but most firms insisted that a common set of assumptions be used by all divisions to avoid inconsistent or conflicting plans. These premises about the future business environment were usually approved by the top executives in each firm.

To illustrate the nature of these environmental forecasts or planning premises, the content of a two-page commentary which was sent to each division in a major food company will be reviewed. Data on four subjects were presented in this document, as follows:

1. "Economic Forecasts," including the projected average annual percentage increases in disposable personal income, food consumption expenditures, and grocery store sales,
2. "Population," including growth rates and absolute numerical forecasts of the United States population in total and for various age groups for the years 1965 and 1970,
3. "Inflationary Trends," including assumptions on the relation of prices and costs, and
4. "Taxes," including known changes in future tax rates.

The Economics Division of one petroleum company published a manual entitled "The Economic Environment for Long-Range Planning" which was sent to each key manager in the company. Periodically, it was revised by sections.

In a large diversified-products corporation, ten-year economic forecasts made by private economists and external groups were compiled by the Marketing Services staff into a manual called "The Business Outlook and World Review, 1965-1975," and it was distributed among the managers of each operating unit for use in long-range planning.

General Electric Company had a group of analysts who considered broad patterns of environmental change over extended time periods. A brief description of this forecasting activity is cited.

> The (Technical Military Planning) TEMPO organization . . . provides General Electric with a special "think" laboratory whose specialists study the world environment to anticipate society's needs five to 25 years in the future.[2]

The predictions of such a group should have important implications for planning long-range commercial activities.

The Market Research Department in one company made forecasts of consumer buying habits and market changes for several future years. These predictions and the results of market and consumer surveys on new products were included in a guidance booklet which was used for preparing five-year plans.

Similar studies were also reported by other companies. The Product Planning Department in one firm made demand forecasts by products and markets for the industry and for the company for each of the next ten years. These forecasts and corresponding sales data for the past ten years were compiled into a reference manual, and the forecasts were revised and extended every year. The time span of these product demand forecasts was increased from five years to ten years in this company in 1963. The Vice President—Product Planning—stated that the longer-term projections would be continued as long as they were reasonably accurate.

Another company reported that their product-by-product demand forecasts had been extended from three years to five years in order to provide data for a new five-year planning procedure. The marketing staff prepared the forecasts in this firm.

The Market Planning staff of a highly diversified manufacturing firm compiled a detailed set of historical market data, without demand projections, and sent it to the key executives in various operating units for use in long-range planning. This manual was entitled "Gross Functional Market for 1071 Products," and it was structured around the standard product classifications of the United States Department of Commerce. This document included data for each of the past few years on:

1. the size of the total market for each functional product,
2. the total "excluded market" for each functional product, or that part of a given market which was served by a type of product not sold by the company, and
3. the market for current company product lines for all United States manufacturers, for all importers, and for the company, respectively.

Each division in the company was expected to predict the future demand for its products, after considering the historical performance record, the existing potential, the economic environment, and the planned strategies for changing the fraction of the market it could serve.

LIMITATIONS OF FORECASTING

Even though many companies and external groups were engaged in extensive economic and market forecasting activities, some of the results seemed to have limited usefulness in corporation long-range planning.

One Vice President reported that macro-economic forecasts were made by staff economists in his firm, but that divisional forecasts of developments in technology and competition were the keys to planning success.

The Director of Corporate Planning in a container manufacturing company said that variations in crop production caused more change in the demand for his company's products than a major depression.

The Head of Commercial Research in another company stated that general economic forecasts were never applied to his firm's business activities, but had possible application when seeking funds in the money markets.

Another Vice President indicated that forecasts of general economic activity in major market areas were not taken into consideration very much in his firm. He said that market research data were based on the expected average demand over a long period of time, and that his company did not speculate on quarterly or yearly fluctuations.[3] A consulting economist provided forecasts to this company which were used for short-run planning, but long-range plans were not postponed or revised unless severe changes in economic activity became evident.

Economic forecasting was done on an irregular basis in one company, and apparently it was not entirely satisfactory. This conclusion is based on the fact that a special research program on "forecasting" had been initiated to seek ways to make better forecasts.

The Director of a large Planning and Economics Department said that economic forecasts had not been made long enough in his company to obtain the degree of top management confidence in them that was necessary for effective long-range planning.

In the motor vehicle industry, total product demand is closely related to general economic activity. In considering the limitations of forecasting, an economist in one automobile company reported that the toughest job was to call the "turning point." In the same company, a product planner pointed out a major limitation of market research when he said that "much of it must be discounted, for people change their minds."

Even though forecasting techniques leave much to be desired, they are being improved rapidly. An independent survey among several economists and planners a few years ago indicated general agreement that the use of computers and improved statistics had resulted in more accurate forecasts.[4]

The Vice President of one steel company stated that "forecasting is becoming more of a science and less an art, but it still involves much guessing." He cited the rapid changes in technology as one important reason for inaccurate forecasts. For example, the amount of steel actually required per unit of product during the 1955-1960 period was much less than predicted in the early 1950's. This inaccurate forecast, and the resulting excess production capacity, were due to improvements in product design and materials, even though unit demand projections were accurate. Foreign steel importers also captured part of the market, and this occurrence had not been predicted.

ADVANCED FORECASTING TECHNIQUES

Economic and market forecasting are important elements of corporate long-range planning, and the rapid advancement in mathematical and statistical techniques and electronic computer capabilities can be expected to produce continued improvements in forecasting.

One promising technique is the use of microanalytic simulation models. In such models, complex interactions between micro-economic components such as decision-making units, markets, and goods are formulated. Alternative consumer behaviors are then predicted, along with their probabilities of occurrence, and these results can be related directly to forecasts of product demand.[5]

Another tool of economic analysis which is being refined and extended currently is called "input-output" analysis. "This technique reckons with the intermediate sales and purchases (outputs and inputs) that carry goods and services from industry to industry, from manufacturer to distributor, and on to their final purchaser in the market." [6] Past economic transactions between an increasing number of sectors of the United States economy may become available more rapidly in the future. If so, individual firms can obtain much useful data from this "systems approach" to market analysis for use in forecasting future product demand and for making more precise long-range plans.

A third technique for product demand forecasting utilizes econometric models which relate sales to other economic variables expressed in aggregate terms. Such models are used by an increasing number of business corporations to forecast the sales volume for an entire industry and for individual firms.

Eventually, all three of these forecasting techniques may be evaluated and used by business firms in an effort to make better decisions about future activities.

CORPORATE OBJECTIVES, GOALS, AND STRATEGIES

IMPORTANCE OF SETTING GOALS

Business "objectives" are the desired end results of future business activities. The broadest objectives of nearly every business firm are (1) to provide goods or services which have economic utility, (2) to make a satisfactory profit, and (3) to survive indefinitely as a going concern. A particular firm will often establish more specific objectives which relate to its own products, services, markets, or activities.

Business "goals" are also hoped-for achievements, and the term "goal" is often used interchangeably with "objective." However, several firms reported that "goals" were quantitative targets which often included a specified attainment date, while "objectives" were broader, qualitative expectations.

The formulation of specific objectives and goals must precede the development of detailed strategies, business plans, and budgets in the process of planning, just as planning must precede the other managerial functions of execution and control. An individual or organization must decide what is to be sought before meaningful action plans can be made.

When specific objectives and goals are established for a corporation and for each of its operating units, these targets have a great potential motivational value. Each operating manager can be encouraged to improve his performance by providing him with challenging goals. Such goals can also serve as performance standards if the managers are compensated for their services on the basis of goal realization. If a manager helps develop his own goals, an even greater motivational effect is provided, for this procedure creates a self-imposed obligation to perform.

In addition, goals serve as important standards for evaluating proposed new projects and extensions of current operations. When specific performance goals are established as acceptance criteria before investments are made, potential losses or unsatisfactory profits can usually be avoided.

Goals must be realistic, however, if they are to be more helpful than harmful. "Profit planning," or setting hard-to-reach profit goals, may motivate managers to seek new ways to reduce costs or to increase revenues, but it can be carried too far. One Vice President stated that "forcing unrealistic budgets on divisions has harmed the company, for demanding the impossible has a horrible effect on morale."

A staff specialist in another company also related the harmful consequences of unrealistic goals in these words:

> If the boss says to increase profits, managers will boost up estimates, but performance often does not meet expectations. The result is often alibis, excuses (some valid), criticism, conflicts between line and staff personnel, and poor morale.

This person believed that setting targets actually forced managers to perform better, but he felt that the goals should be attainable.

Ideally, goals should be established which will contribute to the long-run objectives of the business firm—survival and a satisfactory rate of earnings on the owner's equity. However, such hoped-for results (targets) should be selected only after careful analysis of what is necessary, what is possible, and what is desirable. In the future, more sophisticated planning methods may include such multi-level goal-setting, as well as the assignment or calculation of probabilities of realization for each different goal. Such a refinement, if accompanied by frequent periodic reviews of results and adjustment of goals in the light of new information, would be a valuable aid to decision-making in short-range and long-range planning.

In a complex business enterprise, there are many implicit or explicit goals or objectives, and they vary widely in scope, precision, functional relevance, and time horizon. Therefore, the broad spectrum of objectives and goals should be interrelated so they are reinforcing instead of conflicting. This is one important task that integrated planning can fulfill, for separate operating units in a large firm often develop conflicting goals. If corporate and divisional objectives and goals are clearly defined in writing, any conflicts in the ends sought or in goal interpretation can be more easily detected and resolved.

NATURE OF CORPORATE OBJECTIVES

The objectives of the companies which were investigated were typically very broad and general, if they were made explicit at all. The planning advisor in one electrical equipment firm stated that "general objectives are written, but they are the broad 'creed-type' and are not very useful for business planning or analysis." An individual in another firm reported that "objectives are not written, but informal ones are stated by the President." A third person implied that formal objectives were not firmly established in his company when he said that "corporate objectives may be developed by the corporate head and stated in a speech, sometimes as a result of 'hell-raising' by a major stockholder." Others indicated that the top executives in their firms had never taken the time to formalize objectives.

Most of the companies which provided information on corporate objectives did not have explicit written objectives. The implication of this condition was clearly stated by one Director of Long-Range Planning in these words:

> Many problems in planning have their roots in unclear objectives, for they have not been resolved with the degree of precision needed to set plans on them. They are difficult to form—either from the abstract or from experience—and executives differ in their personal views of profit and growth objectives.

This planner added that more effort would be given to objective formulation in his firm in the future, and he expected the Corporate Planning Department to have an active role in this effort.

One company reported that corporate objectives were not written so they would not be made known to the firm's competitors.

The need for more specific corporate objectives to serve as a basis for long-range planning was implied or stated by several persons, but very few companies reported that detailed objectives had been developed. In one firm, the Director of Corporate Planning had compiled a list of 18 corporate objectives under the guidance of top executives. He indicated that the objectives were hard to "sell," however, for the division managers could not visualize (as yet) the relationship between these objectives and the task of developing specific long-range operational plans. Their attitude toward the objectives seemed to be—"so what."

Corporate objectives were also developed in another company after an analysis of the business environment was completed during the planning process. These objectives pertained to marketing, supply (make or buy considerations), and product development.

NATURE OF CORPORATE GOALS

In spite of the scarcity of meaningful qualitative corporate objectives, many firms did report some kind of existing quantitative goals. These goals were stated most often in terms of dollar earnings per share of common stock or absolute dollar earnings in some future period of time.

Rate-of-return goals (earnings/asset value) were frequently mentioned, and some companies set such goals, as well as profit goals, for each division in the company. One firm reported that a corporation rate-of-return goal of 7 per cent (after taxes) had been in effect for years and that all divisions tried to achieve it. Several companies indicated that the rate-of-return goal varied between divisions, and was generally higher for new investment proposals than for an extension of existing operations.

Some companies stressed that their goal was to maximize corporation earnings, but not necessarily the earnings for a given division. To achieve this goal, profitable divisional plans might be sacrificed to benefit the corporation. One company was considering an evaluation method to determine the extent to which each operating unit acted in the best interest of the company, even if divisional or departmental results were harmed.

Goals were assigned to each division of one firm in dollar units of income before taxes. In other companies, the divisions set their own goals for sales in dollars, profits in dollars, and rate of return on the dollar value of assets utilized. These goals were then approved by a top management committee. In one company in which division managers set their own goals, the Corporate Development Department and the Profit Improvement Committee had developed and recommended specific goals to each division.

In a petroleum company which developed ten-year plans, goals were set in terms of the volume of petroleum to be produced and sold, the level of capital expenditures, and the amount of net income.

Growth goals were also frequently expressed, usually in terms of sales or profits. However, one firm stated such goals in terms of manpower growth (increase in number of employees) and production efficiency.

White Motor Corporation established five-year goals (fifth year targets) for earnings per share, total sales, profit margin, and market share. They announced specific numerical corporation goals for these four criteria of performance, and also for sales and market share of specific product groups. President John N. Bauman considers it a challenge to let outsiders know internal plans.[7]

Market share goals (per cent of industry sales) were also established in several companies. These goals and other quantitative goals were often set for each year of the next five years, and usually were higher in successive years.

NATURE OF CORPORATE STRATEGIES

Business strategy is a broad plan of action which is expected to achieve previously-set objectives and goals, if subsequent detailed plans of implementation are developed and effected properly. Most of the companies which were investigated did not have written strategic plans, but a considerable amount of strategic planning was done.

Millard H. Pryor, Jr., Director of Product Policy in The Singer Company, believed that strategic planning should include three major considerations, especially in regard to international business. He stated that these essential elements of strategic planning were "the extent of geographical involvement, the time horizon, and the allocation of resources."

The strategy of a business firm with respect to geographical involvement may vary widely. For example, The Singer Company had chosen to market its products in every part of the world which was politically "open." Other companies may choose to conduct business in only a few developed or underdeveloped nations, markets, or regions. Mr. Pryor also pointed out that the involvement may be based on either offensive or defensive marketing strategy in each of the markets selected.

The time horizon for a given business activity was also considered an important element of strategy. Usually, a particular market is serviced or a given product is sold for an indefinite continuous period of time. However, an opportunistic strategy may be employed where a finite involvement time of two, five, or ten years is expected.

Resource allocation, the third element of strategy discussed by Mr. Pryor, is a vital consideration. Decisions on horizontal versus vertical integration and on partial versus complete ownership may be involved. Also, the strategic allocation of funds will determine the expediture level for research, product development, and advertising. This type of allocation is sometimes called tactical planning, but it may also be an important element of strategy.

In one electrical equipment manufacturing company, "strategic spending" was an important topic of discussion in a procedure manual which was sent to each division for use in preparing a "Profit Plan." Strategic expenditures were defined as those "to enhance the future strength of the company and its ability to compete profitably." Any expenditure which was not required for current operations was included in this category, and the earnings which resulted from such spending were not expected until future years. This firm incurred strategic expeditures for activities to develop or improve products, to develop markets, to increase production or marketing efficiency, and to increase production capacity.

This type of spending was essential for continued long-run success. However, it reduced current earnings significantly at times, since it was customary to record many of these expenditures fully in the current accounting period. This presented a dilemma for the division or department managers who were responsible for the performance of profit centers. These managers were evaluated on the basis of current earnings, but such earnings were reduced by strategic spending. On the other hand, the same persons were responsible for forward planning and strategic action to insure continued earnings in future periods.

In an effort to guide these managers, the planning manual stated that "each Division should strive for the proper balance between current profit margins and investment in the future of the business." This admonition was not helpful in achieving the desired balance, but it served as a useful reminder that a balance was necessary.

The strategic plan of one large electronics equipment company was unique among the companies which were studied. This plan contained six major elements of strategy:

1. increase manpower by 15 per cent in X years,
2. improve production efficiency so that total corporate growth exceeds 15 per cent,
3. seek and develop products and markets to utilize the projected manpower growth,
4. utilize existing technology in product development to the extent possible, instead of seeking new knowledge through investment in basic research,
5. continue business activities with the present type of products, but be alert for opportunities to diversify and make acquisitions or other investments, and
6. provide the necessary financing for the preceding strategic plans.

In this company, manpower was considered the limiting factor for growth. This variable was critical because of (1) the restricted capacity of the existing organization for training new employees, (2) the required training time, and (3) the limitations of the labor supply.

Summary—Objective, Goal, and Strategy Formulation

Objectives, goals, and strategies varied in content and in the degree of formalization in the companies which were studied. Many of these business corporations apparently had not formulated specific long-range goals and alternative approaches for achieving them. Very few explicit statements of objectives or strategies were reported.

However, there seemed to be a growing awareness of the importance of more systematic long-range planning and of the essential role of carefully-formulated objectives in such planning. Therefore, companies in increasing numbers are expected to make a greater effort to develop explicit objectives, goals, and strategies in the future. This task will probably be assigned to corporate planning staffs who will work under the guidance of top executives. Divisional goals and strategies will also be formalized in more companies through the joint efforts of divisional managers and staff specialists.

Footnotes for Chapter 2

[1] William F. May, "Effective Management—Meeting the Challenge of Change," An address before the 33rd National Packaging Conference, New York, N. Y., April 20, 1964.

[2] *1964 Annual Report—General Electric* (New York: General Electric Company, 1965), p. 20.

[3] Other companies were also concerned primarily about the trend and average level of demand, because a few of them reported the use of a two-point projection (based on 1970 and 1975 demand forecasts, for example) instead of year-by-year forecasts.

[4] Ted Stanton, "Sounder Spending? Improved Forecasting Tools Guide Today's Capital Outlays," *The Wall Street Journal,* June 25, 1964, p. 10.

[5] This technique is explained by Guy H. Orcutt in "Microanalytic Models of Socioeconomic Systems: A New Approach to Forecasting," *Papers Presented to the Ninth Annual Conference on the Economic Outlook at The University of Michigan* (Ann Arbor: The University of Michigan, 1961), pp. 64–74.

[6] Wassily W. Leontief, "The Structure of the U. S. Economy," *Scientific American,* CCXII, No. 4 (April, 1965), 25.

[7] "Into the Big Time," *Forbes,* XCV, No. 4 (February 15, 1965), 29.

Chapter 3

Formalized Long-Range Planning Practices

In any organized group, activities should be conducted in a standardized manner and in a logical sequence to insure efficient attainment of goals. Among the companies which were investigated, those with highly formalized planning systems had developed specific administrative procedures for long-range planning. These procedures provided a vital "mechanism" for converting business opportunities, organization capabilities, and corporation goals into tangible plans for future activities. Therefore, to understand more fully how the process of long-range planning actually worked in practice, the procedures utilized by several of these corporations are reviewed in the first part of this chapter.

ADMINISTRATIVE PROCEDURES FOR DEVELOPING LONG-RANGE PLANS

NATURE OF INSTRUCTIONS FOR FORMAL LONG-RANGE PLANNING

The first step in the administrative process of formal long-range planning was the preparation and distribution of instructions by corporate staffs to the operating units for use in developing specific plans. In some companies, broad corporate strategies, policies, or goals were included, but the instructions or guides were primarily concerned with:

1. the content of plans,
2. formats, definitions, and assumptions (to seek uniformity between divisional plans and to permit consolidation into a corporate plan), and
3. sequential procedures, responsibility assignments, and completion dates for each step in the planning cycle.

However, the planning instructions which different companies had developed varied considerably in format and scope. They reflected the nature of a particular business, the basic approach and philosophy of long-range planning in each company, and the orientation of the person or group that prepared them.

Planning Instructions in American Machine and Foundry Company

A concise 17-page manual developed by the American Machine and Foundry Company (AMF) contained specific sequential steps for long-range planning at the divisional level. This manual, called the "Business Unit Planning Guide," provided a broad frame of reference for such planning by reviewing the objectives, hierarchy of plans, and essential elements in the AMF planning program.

Penetrating questions such as the following ones were included in this guide: "What do we want to be, what changes will be required, and how will we accomplish this? Where have we been, where are we, what do we face over the next five to ten years, and where will we be if we continue as we have been?"

The planning manual indicated that the business plan for each major operating unit in the company should include a statement of broad objectives or purpose, specific long-range goals, a strategic plan, and detailed action programs. Each action program in the long-range plan for one operating unit was expected to contain:

1. the objective of the program,
2. a specific quantitative goal or target to be reached in a given time,
3. background information on the relation of the program to operating

unit, group, and corporation goals, current operations, and external conditions,

4. a review of alternative programs considered,
5. a description of the major aspects of the proposed program, as well as methods of implementation, a time-table for activities, responsibility assignments, planning criteria, assumptions, judgmental areas, and critical factors for success,
6. a set of financial data, including pro forma profit and loss statements, capital investment requirements, and cash flow schedules, and
7. program control methods, such as a time schedule or procedures for interim measurement and review.

A program summary form was illustrated in the planning guide, and it provided for the classification of each proposed program as either exploratory, for maintenance of markets, for cost reduction, for product quality improvement, or for new product development. This form was also designed so that the probability of success for each program could be indicated in one of four probability ranges.

The specific outlines, questions, and formats contained in the AMF planning guide made it a very useful reference manual for long-range planning. This set of instructions did not include a time schedule for various planning activities, or detailed formats for financial summaries, or directions about the mechanics of plan preparation and routing. However, these additional instructions could be included in a separate document.

Planning Instructions in a Major Food Company

The Controller's Office in one large food corporation prepared a set of detailed instructions for use by the operating divisions in developing plans for the next three fiscal years. These instructions included:

1. a timetable for eleven specific planning steps (extending from November to March),
2. the changes made in accounting techniques and concepts since the preceding planning cycle,
3. economic assumptions,
4. definitions and directions for preparing nine financial and research project forms,
5. guidelines for preparing comments on specific long-range plans, including a list of external and internal factors which might have a major impact on planned divisional activities,
6. technical instructions pertaining to reproduction methods and the required number of copies of each completed form, and
7. directions for preparing photographic slides for a summary presenta-

tion of each division's long-range plans to the Operating Policy Committee.

Sample copies of the nine forms which each major operating unit was required to complete were provided with the planning instructions to the Controller in each division. These forms were entitled:

1. Profit and Loss Statements—Fiscal 196__ to Fiscal 196__ (pro forma, for current year and 3 future years),
2. Significant Adjustments to Profit and Loss Statements,
3. Major Research Projects—New Products and Idea Development,
4. Major Research Projects—Product and Process Improvement,
5. Major Research Projects—New Identified Products,
6. Major Research Projects—Pioneering Information Research,
7. Major Research Projects—Other Miscellaneous Research,
8. Statement of Return Rates, Funds Employed and Company Investment, and Transfers of Funds Employed, and
9. Salaried Manpower—Salaries, Wages, and Benefits.

For the summary presentation of long-range plans to the Operating Policy Committee, slides of 11 charts were required. Most of them were designed as seven-year bar graphs which included data on operating variables for each of the past three years, the current year, and each of the next three years. The chart titles were:

1. Trend Summary (of volume, net sales, and profits before taxes),
2. Volume (in dollars and per cent annual change),
3. Net sales (in dollars and per cent annual change),
4. Gross Profit (in dollars and as a per cent of net sales),
5. Profit Before Tax (in dollars and per cent annual change),
6. Origin of Profit Before Tax (in dollars for established products, and for new products, less development expenses),
7. Source of Profit Before Tax Change,
8. Funds—Return on Funds,
9. Inventories,
10. Capital Program,
11. Salaried Manpower and Salaries, Wages, and Benefits.

Sample copies of each chart were also attached to the planning instructions.

This set of instructions was carefully designed to provide a uniform procedure for divisional long-range planning. The focus was on financial planning and control, but major research projects were given special emphasis. There was also adequate provision for commentaries and major planning assumptions to support specific plans for new products, marketing programs, or investment proposals. The analytical framework provided in these instructions was not nearly as detailed as the one in the American Machine and Foundry Company's "Business Unit Planning Guide" which was discussed in the preceding section. However, the methods of presenting financial plans and the procedural directions were more detailed in the planning instructions of the food company. Therefore, a combination of these two sets of instructions would provide a very broad and sound foundation for effective corporate long-range planning.

CORPORATE STAFF REVIEW OF DIVISIONAL PLANS

In companies where formalized long-range planning was decentralized to the operating units, specific plans were developed by personnel in each major organizational unit after they received the planning instructions. These business unit plans were usually combined into divisional or group plans and submitted to the corporate planning or finance staffs (or both) for review and consolidation.

Long-range plans were approved by operating managers at the divisional or group level before they were submitted to the corporate staff specialists. However, planning specialists at the lower levels were usually in close contact with the corporate staffs while plans were being developed. After the plans reached the corporate staff groups, they were reviewed for internal consistency, completeness, feasibility, and for inter-divisional compatibility. Staff recommendations for revision or acceptance of different parts of a given plan were made to a top executive or to a corporation planning committee. However, planners in several companies stressed the importance of discussing their recommendations with the manager of the affected operating unit before making a report to top management.

One Vice President with responsibility for planning said that "you don't surprise the divisions on proposed changes." A Director of Business Planning stated that "continuous staff consultation prevents the military court-martial type of review where people are defensive and fear criticism." Thus, a close working relationship between the corporate planning staff and operating managers seemed to be one essential for effective formalized long-range planning.

Another Director of Corporate Planning said that "the President can't tell a General Manager he has to work with the Corporate Planning Department, but rather the group must earn its spurs by helping the Division." He added that "the corporate staff might oppose the divisions on rare occasions, but they (the division managers) knew if plans got through the Planning Department, the chances of acceptance were better than 90 per cent."

TOP EXECUTIVE REVIEW AND APPROVAL OF DIVISIONAL PLANS

The final step in the formal planning procedure in most companies was a review of proposed long-range plans by the President or by a committee of top executives.[1] Usually the operating manager of each division and his staff would present their own plans at review meetings, but the corporate planning staff attended and participated in the discussions. Corporate planners also presented consolidated plans which combined those from each operating unit, and they proposed projects, acquisitions, or investments to meet corporate goals which extended beyond those of any division.

Changes in some aspect of the proposed plans were often made after these review meetings. The key corporate planning coordinator served as the secretary of the top planning committee in some companies, and this assignment enabled him to record and follow up on proposed changes in the plans. One effective administrative technique was reported by a Director of Corporate Planning who served as the review committee secretary. He included the name of each person responsible for changing a plan or providing additional data, and also the assigned completion date, in the minutes of the meeting (even if such details were agreed upon after the meeting).

The Board of Directors reviewed and gave final approval to long-range plans in some companies, especially for major capital spending proposals. However, the most common type of Board review was a brief slide presentation to keep the directors informed.

The procedure for approval of long-range plans in one large decentralized company was outlined by a corporate planning advisor in these words:

> The plan is summarized on prescribed forms which indicate the resources required and the expected results. These forms are reviewed by Divisional General Managers and Group Executives and summarized to show Division and Company totals. During these reviews (1) immediate approval may be given, (2) the need for specific revisions may be indicated, (3) the requested resources may be denied, or (4) improved (projected) operating results may be requested. In the latter examples, a revised plan is prepared and subsequently approved and implemented.

This planning advisor was a member of the corporate Controller's staff, and he reviewed the long-range plans with each Group Executive to point out any inconsistencies or improper accounting procedures. The President then met with the Group Executives and discussed ways to reduce capital spending proposals if they exceeded available funds or a desired spending level. However, this step was necessary only one time during the past several years, since capital funds were generally considered to be unlimited.[2] Usually, the President permitted Group Executives to approve their respective long-range plans. However, the Board of Directors approved or disapproved each capital appropriation of $500,000 or more.

PROCEDURES FOR CENTRALIZED LONG-RANGE PLANNING

The planning function was centralized in a few of the companies which were studied, and the procedure for long-range planning in one of these firms was described as follows:

> A given plan is developed by Market Development (Department) taking the lead and either outlining some particular strategy or corporate development plans or informational requirements for operational planning. These preliminary ideas are presented to those concerned (in the operating units) for modification and improvement. When redrafted, the plans are reviewed by the President for his modification and approval.

In a major steel corporation where planning was centralized to a high degree, the first step in developing long-range plans was to forecast the product demand for future years, using the procedure outlined in chapter 2. After calculating the tonnage needed in each sales district to provide the "target" fraction of the total forecasted demand, the optimum production level for each area was determined. A computer program which incorporated the projected demand, existing production capacity, freight costs, etc., was utilized for this purpose.

Whenever the optimum production rate in each area was found, the additional facilities needed to produce the desired tonnage were specified. Then the capital costs for the necessary equipment, buildings, and layout were estimated by the Chief Engineer of the corporation and various district engineers. Alternative plans for achieving company goals were also developed for some areas, and investment proposals were formulated after considering the amount of available capital and the company debt policy. The Vice President who was responsible for long-range planning recommended certain plans to the President, and after the top executives and the Board of Directors reviewed alternative plans, they made the necessary decisions about future activities.

In another steel company, a different planning procedure was followed. In each division of the firm, a planning committee was appointed to assist the division manager in gathering data and preparing capital investment plans. A Corporation Planning Committee coordinated the efforts of the committees at lower levels and combined their recommendations. A corporate staff specialist served as the Director of Forward Planning and as chairman of the Corporate Planning Committee. He also developed long-range plans for review by this committee.

In this planning system, functional specialists at all levels developed operational plans, while the corporate planning staff evaluated the effect of technological and market developments and coordinated all planning activities. The Management Executive Committee reviewed and approved corporate plans for capital investment.

PROCEDURES FOR CAPITAL INVESTMENT PLANNING

One of the most important elements of long-range planning was that of deciding on future capital investments—their nature, cost, timing, and expected benefits. In each of the companies which had formalized its planning procedures, the strategic and operational plans which were developed to meet broad objectives or specific goals usually culminated in proposals to invest additional capital. The procedures for reviewing and deciding on such proposals were a vital and clearly-defined part of the broader long-range planning procedures.

In some companies, capital investment planning was a separate and distinct part of long-range planning. Even in firms which had no formalized planning system, facilities planning or capital budgeting was always formalized to some extent and was the primary focal point of "informal" long-range planning.

Limitations of the "Rate of Return" Criterion

The allocation of limited funds among competing alternative projects was a critical part of the planning procedure and one of the most difficult. Investments in production facilities had to be made several months or years in advance of any expected return, and the uncertainties of future technology, markets, prices, costs, and competing products created a considerable amount of risk. These factors made accurate appraisal of the potential value of alternative investments very difficult, if not impossible.

Most companies required some minimum expected rate of return on proposed investments, but if the total cost of acceptable projects exceeded the available or designated funds, priority was given to the most urgent or most promising projects. Then the result was sometimes "bickering, turmoil, and replanning" among the managers whose projects were rejected or postponed.

Some companies used the "discounted cash flow" method for measuring the expected rate of return in an effort to make more accurate evaluations of investment proposals. However, one of the very largest corporations did not use this method because "the input data on future demand and other variables is too inaccurate." A staff specialist in another company reported that a system existed in his firm for allocating capital on the basis of rates of return which were determined by the "discounted cash flow" method. However, he said that in actual practice, the "degree of reasonableness" of a spending proposal and the "competence of the manager involved" were the deciding factors.

A Unique Capital Allocation System

The company mentioned in the preceding section which did not use the "present value" criterion in calculating rates of return had also abandoned "rate of return" as the primary basis for allocating capital or for evaluating performance. This action was taken in the mid-1950's. However, rates of return on proposed investments were currently calculated and reported for secondary consideration. In place of the commonly used rate-of-return criterion, this corporation utilized a unique system in which the criterion for investment was *not* the merit of the proposal. Instead, the past performance of the manager who made the proposal was the critical factor.

Profitability was the major evaluation criterion in this system. It was measured largely in terms of residual income (net income minus a fixed percentage of the value of the assets employed), the ratio of net income to net sales billed, and investment turnover. Profitability standards were set for each operating unit, and those that achieved at least 90 per cent of their budgeted profit on existing investments were permitted to invest more funds (up to a specified amount for each managerial level) without higher approval. If a given unit manager failed to meet this performance standard, future proposals had to go one level higher than normal in the management hierarchy for approval.

This method of capital allocation was considered to be effective by the company because managers were motivated to be more exact and conscientious in their planning efforts. They also tried to improve operating performance by cost control or revenue-producing activities in order to avoid the status of "non-qualification."

This was the same company where funds were generally available for all capital investment proposals, as discussed in a preceding section. However, a detailed five-page proposal and financial summary form had to be filled out and submitted when a specific capital appropriation request was made. At this time, each request was reviewed carefully by representatives of the corporate Controller and by the corporate manufacturing, marketing, and engineering staffs.

Another procedure which "encouraged" long-range planning in this firm was the requirement that annual operating budget proposals contain projected capital spending levels for several future years. These projections were requested from operating managers for each of several classes of capital expenditures, such as equipment, buildings, land, leases, etc.

Another decentralized company followed a capital allocation procedure which was somewhat similar to the one just described, but the consequences of poor performance were more drastic. A unit manager was authorized to spend a given number of dollars as he saw fit and whenever he chose. In a year or two, if he hadn't produced as expected, he was "lopped off" and replaced. The Director of Planning in this company stated that "the 'casualty' rate has been high, even among vice presidents."

Other Investment Planning Procedures

In one company where formal "Profit Plans" for the coming three years were developed by each operating unit, a separate procedure was established for capital investment planning. The instructions for this activity were entitled "Planning and Control of Facilities Expenditures." During the planning period, each major operating unit in the firm prepared a proposed "Facilities Program" in which they projected facilities expenditures for three years. They also detailed the projects which were planned for the coming year. These proposals were then reviewed by a Capital Expenditures Committee composed of top executives and "the Facilities Programs were adjusted, if necessary, to bring their total within the amount of available funds."

The recommendations of this committee were submitted to the President and to the Board of Directors for acceptance. After the approval of proposed programs, specific capital appropriations were made as requested according to a prescribed pattern of spending authorization. A formal change in this procedure was initiated a few years ago to reduce the planning period from five to three years. This was done because "experience has indicated that three years is the maximum period for meaningful projections."

Many of the participating companies projected capital spending plans for five years, and these data were often included in long-range plans. However, they were not as detailed as capital appropriation requests which sought authorization to spend funds for capital projects. An allocation of capital among operating units was made in some companies when the five-year plans were approved, and this served as the effective capital budget for future periods up to two and one-half years in length.

Many companies have been forced to ration capital, especially in the last few years of continuous high economic activity, and this restriction has caused cancellation or deferral of many projects. In one company, a committee of executives questioned each Division Manager about the impact of deferral of proposed investments on profits, implementation costs, and other variables when they reviewed his long-range plans.

In some companies, annual capital budgets were submitted by operating units for executive review, adjustment, and approval. These budgets generally corresponded to the data in the first year of the firm's five-year plan. However, one company included only funds for normal operating needs such as equipment replacements and excluded the capital needed for growth.

When capital proposals were reviewed in another company, the capital spending projections for more distant years were not reduced to the expected "possible" level. However, for the coming year, they were "pruned" down to the total permissible level of capital expenditure. This procedure produced in effect an annual capital budget. It also permitted optimistic planning by operating divisions for future periods by avoiding a decision to reject or defer a project until it was necessary to do so.

RELATION OF LONG-RANGE AND SHORT-RANGE PLANNING

Long-range and short-range planning were becoming more highly integrated in the companies which were studied as planning procedures became more formalized. In many of these companies, the operating and capital budgets, or a combined budget, for the coming year were identical or very similar to the financial projections for the first year of a three-, four-, or five-year plan. However, in the companies where the budget figures and the plan projections corresponded, the data in the budgets were somewhat more detailed.

Budget proposals were usually submitted after long-range plans were approved. The Vice President—Planning—in one company stated that whenever proposed budgets differed from the plans, meetings were held to resolve such deviations. Since budgets should be financial expressions of plans, it is logical that they evolve from and accurately reflect approved plans. By insisting that budgets and plans were in agreement, top management indicated to lower-level managers that planning was important and should be done carefully.

FREQUENCY OF REVISION OF LONG-RANGE PLANS

Most companies which developed formal long-range plans revised them each year, adding one year and deleting one year. One Director of Planning reported that a ten-year plan which was developed in his company was revised every other year, and "patched" in between. Another company made a detailed revision of its five-year plans about the fourth year, but reviewed and adjusted them every year. Some firms reviewed plans every six months and made revisions due to changes in demand, prices, operating costs, and other factors.

An electronics and office equipment company initiated quarterly reviews of its long-range plans a few years ago. Five-year plans became twenty-period plans. Revisions were made each quarter to reflect recent developments, and the budget was reviewed, revised if necessary, and approved for the next quarter.

This procedure provided significant benefits to the company. It permitted greater flexibility and also minimized excessive spending which a fixed annual budget tended to encourage. Planning and evaluation became a continuous function for operating managers and staff personnel alike, and the work load of the Profit Improvement Committee was spread more evenly over the entire year. Thus, the new procedure had considerable merit. An evaluation of past performance was also made during these periodic reviews to determine the reasons for deviations from financial plans. This follow-up action was expected to lead to more careful short-range and long-range planning.

Pattern of Change in Business Planning Systems

In reviewing long-range planning procedures in 45 large corporations, a trend toward more formalized planning systems was clearly evident. However, the rate of change was not as rapid as might be expected, for a long period of training and evolution was necessary to alter patterns of thought and action. Several planning specialists expressed the belief that at least three years were required to introduce a formal planning system and to obtain the active interest and involvement of operating managers. Changes seemed to be more rapid whenever a new chief executive was elected who subsequently introduced a philosophy of management in which systematic planning was an integral part.

NATURE OF WRITTEN LONG-RANGE PLANS

The culmination of long-range planning activities in the companies which had formal planning systems was the preparation of a written long-range corporate plan. All planning did not cease at this time, however, for it was a continual process of evaluating company progress, forecasting changes in the business environment, and replanning. Nevertheless, the long-range plan was a central focal point for much of the effort expended in long-range planning. Therefore, the nature of long-range plans which various companies had developed will be discussed in the following section.

Size and Time Span of Long-Range Plans

One Vice President stated that a long-range plan "might be six file cases of material in total, a two- or three-inch thick book at the Vice Presidential level, and then only 30 minutes worth of slides or charts at the Board of Directors' level." This description would fit the pattern found in most companies that prepared formal plans. However, the amount of raw data (statistical tables, descriptions, and drawings) would vary with the nature of the plans.

Long-range plans varied in the span of time covered from three years to 20, with some plans extending four, five, seven, and ten years. However, most of the plans were for five years, and the one company that looked ahead for 20 years projected most financial statements for only ten to 15 years.

CONTENT OF LONG-RANGE PLANS

The most common elements in all of the plans reviewed were projections of net income and capital expenditures for each year of the period considered. Net income projections were typically made on pro forma profit and loss statements, and in some companies, they were made on the same type of forms as control budgets. Such statements usually included the dollar amount of revenue expected from each product or product group and market area. They also included the dollar amount of expected expenses of various types and the residual net income.

These data were compiled for each profit center or basic operating unit [3] in a company as a general rule, and were then combined and condensed for successively higher organizational units such as divisions and groups, and finally for the entire corporation. Projected sales volumes were given for several product and market categories and the expected selling prices were included to provide the basis for revenue data. Anticipated changes in net income from one period to the next were often indicated, along with the reasons for such expected changes.

Cash flow statements were also commonly projected to aid in financial management. With such projections, the amount of external funds needed in each future time period could be predicted. In addition, plans could be made for using any surplus funds which were expected.

In some long-range plans, projected balance sheets for each of the next few years were included.

The amount of supporting data for financial projections in many of these plans was quite extensive. Detailed descriptions, outlines, and diagrams were included, as well as statements of objectives, goals, and strategies. These documents really constituted the "heart" of a long-range plan. The mere extension of past financial performance into furture periods was generally a useless exercise unless the data were supported by carefully-drawn business plans. Financial projections without careful analysis and planning had led to grossly inaccurate expectations in some companies.

One petroleum company made five-year financial projections for current activities to show what could be expected without planning or improvement, and then made similar ten-year projections which were called the "optimistic forecast" to show what might be realized. Some of the "gap" between the two projections depended on oil discoveries, but much of it could be closed by better management. Thus, a psychological stimulus to planning was provided.

The focal point for developing plans was usually the projected sales volume of new and existing products and services. An analysis of the end markets, as in the procedure outlined in chapter 2 for forecasting the demand for steel, was often included in the plans.

In some companies, a two-dimensional matrix was developed which related each type of product the company produced, or expected to produce, to each existing or potential type of market. For each possible product-market intersection, the total size of the market and the company's share of the market were estimated. Market-share goals were then set and plans were developed for increasing the company's share of various markets for particular products. One company listed products in four groups—current lines, positively necessary future lines, likely new lines, and possible new lines.

In some plans, market data in physical or monetary units were also included which compared the company's share of various markets to the share of each competitor and to the total existing and potential market. Pricing trends and the strategy of principal competitors were also included in the long-range plans of a few companies.

Each division in some companies was requested to define the scope of the unit's activities in its long-range plan. This task was considered difficult, but it was necessary in order to avoid inefficiency or harmful inter-divisional competition.

Other types of detailed analyses were included in various plans, but the instructions of one corporate planning staff to the company's operating units contained an excellent criterion for deciding what to include in a long-range plan. Each division manager was told that data should not be included in his plans unless it would be useful to him in running his part of the business.

For the capital investment proposals in most long-range business plans, written justifications were required. Possible alternative actions were sometimes described, and rate-of-return analyses were usually included. If a new production facility was proposed, the reasons for the selecting of a given plant location, such as nearness to markets, low wage rates, or other factors, were included in the plan. Detailed engineering and market research data were also given, but such data were not as complete as when specific appropriations were requested.

ORGANIZATION OF LONG-RANGE PLANS

Long-range plans were organized in various ways in different companies. In one company, each profit center developed four "principal" types of plans. These pertained to product lines, manufacturing operations, functional marketing, and research and development. Several "derivative" plans were also formulated—for administration and control, organization and personnel, facilities, and finances. These secondary plans were essential for implementation of the "principal" plans, for elements such as finances or personnel might be a limiting factor in effecting the basic plans. In this company, all plans pertained to a future time period of five years except the research and development plans, which were for seven to ten years.

Even though various long-range business plans differed in their formats, many of them contained essentially the same type of information. The table of contents from a "Five-year Business Plan" which was developed by one division of a large corporation is shown in Table 3 to illustrate the content

TABLE 3

OUTLINE OF A "FIVE-YEAR BUSINESS PLAN"
PREPARED BY A DIVISION OF ONE CORPORATION

Section	*Topic*
I	Business Results Summary
	Operations
	Business Indices
	Marketing
	Product
	Costs and Productivity
	Facilities
	Personnel
	Product Line Performance
II	Business Environment
III	Division Guidelines
IV	Most Important Problems and Opportunities
V	Business Strategy
VI	Major Business Plans and Programs
VII	Business Results
Appendix I	Product Line Analyses and Plans
Appendix II	Cost Analyses and Plans

and organization of a well designed long-range plan.

Another more detailed outline of an excellent "Mission Plan" is reproduced in Table 4, chapter 4. This framework for long-range plans was developed and used by the International Minerals and Chemical Corporation. For summarizing objectives and goals in its long-range plan, Motorola Inc. utilized a practical grid-type format which is shown in chapter 5, Table 5. The organization of functional and financial plans in a major automobile company is described in chapter 6.

GENERAL APPRAISAL

Some divisions and companies spent much more time and effort than others in developing meaningful plans, but the results in these organizations were expected to repay the costs many times. Several companies reported that the returns from formalized planning were already evident.

The formal procedures for planning forced managers and staff personnel to think beyond current activities, and thereby led to creative investigation and action. Long-range plans often raised as many questions as they answered.

Written plans provided a firm basis for analysis, discussion, and decision-making. They also served as a continuous planning reference and a standard for evaluation of results. Finally, they remained as a foundation for planning in the next time period.

CURRENT USAGE OF ELECTRONIC COMPUTERS IN LONG-RANGE PLANNING

The capability of electronic computers for solving or simulating complex business problems has increased at a truly remarkable rate since the first commercially-built computer was delivered in 1951. During this period, mathematical and statistical techniques have also been improved and the amount of information available for use in business planning has increased significantly. The applications for computers in business management have multiplied rapidly, so it was not unexpected that the range of uses had extended to long-range planning.

Several of the companies which were contacted reported specific forward-planning applications of electronic computers, while many others indicated that they had not used computers for this purpose. In the following sections, specific planning applications and the prospects for future utilization of computers in long-range planning are reviewed. In addition, the views of some corporation planners who were pessimistic about computerized planning are stated.

APPLICATIONS OF OPERATIONS RESEARCH AND COMPUTERS IN PLANNING

In the International Business Machines Corporation, assistance in evaluating alternative courses of action was given by use of the computer. Programs have been developed for manipulation of planning data and logic, and some dynamic models have been developed of various business functions. Also, a network of systems for obtaining data used in planning has been under development in IBM since 1966. The Corporate Planning Department indicated that "the use of a uniform Fortran-derived language called PSG (Planning System Generator), for operation from Terminals at various locations connected to a central processor, has been instrumental in advancing this development work."

Computers were used to make financial analyses of profitability (rate of return on investments) in another electronics equipment company. A simulation model was used to analyze the profitability of existing and proposed products. This model included variables such as order forecasts, product applications, prices, product mix, manpower utilization, and equipment failure frequency. Decisions to change the product mix or prices might result from such an analysis, and investments in new or expanded facilities might follow.

One large steel company used computer programs in facility planning to determine the optimum production level for each geographical region, as reported in a preceding section.

The Vice President of another steel corporation reported that his firm used computers in many areas of operational planning and indicated that they were an important tool for long-range planning. He thought that his company had gone further than many others with such computer applications, and stated that over 30 specialists (engineers and mathematicians) were assigned to a computer unit.

One petroleum company used computers for planning operational schedules and facilities, and also for analyzing alternative investment opportunities.

A planning group in the General Electric Company utilized computers in long-range planning, as reported in these words:

> The Corporate Planning Operation . . . is charged with assessing the effect on the Company of basic changes in the economy, in living habits, in international trade and in technology. Using computer techniques, the Operation seeks to identify those areas where General Electric can make the best contribution, and recommends plans by which these opportunities can be realized.[4]

In one corporation, computers were used to optimize product distribution patterns, and this application to operational planning had been extended to plant location and facility planning in other companies. A computer application of this type and three other applications in the International Minerals and Chemical Corporation are described in some detail in chapter 4.

Computers were used by a motor vehicle manufacturer to forecast the demand for automobiles and by a petroleum company to forecast the demand for its products. The use of computers for forecasting can be expected to increase rapidly as corporations, universities, and government agencies develop new and improved mathematical and statistical models for this purpose.

One large food processing firm reported that computers had been used internally to a limited extent for planning. A central sales control program was being developed to record and analyze sales to major customers over an extended time period. The results of this analysis (sales volume, profitability level, and trends) were expected to reveal inadequate performance so that plans for improvement could be developed quickly. This system should lead to improved short-range planning, and the cumulative results should also have significant implications for long-range planning.

Marketing models had also been tested in the same company. These models included variables such as prices, elasticity of demand, competitive reaction, and the impact of advertising on sales. The effect on profits of different assumed values for these variables was determined by computerized simulation studies. The value of this type of computer analysis to the company was uncertain, however, for "the answer depends so much on assumptions."

One company was developing a computerized planning system, and the goal of another firm was to program an overall model of the corporation.

Thus, on the basis of inquiries among a limited number of the firms which were investigated, the utilization of electronic computers and operations research techniques for business planning was significant. The applications were of many types and the potential value of these applications to individual firms was great.

VIEWS ON THE LIMITATIONS OF COMPUTERIZED PLANNING

The Manager of Planning in a large petroleum company indicated that his firm had seriously considered a joint program with external specialists for developing models to use internally for computerized planning. However, this program had not materialized, because the estimated cost of one million dollars could not be justified on the basis of expected benefits. Thus, the cost of computerized planning may be prohibitive for some companies.

One planning advisor was very pessimistic about the use of computers in long-range planning. He said that his company had spent ten years and 50 million dollars on operations research, and he felt that it had not been very productive. He believed that in many cases the specialists had failed to develop realistic models because they lacked the knowledge and judgment of managers who were closer to primary company operations. He compared their efforts to the diagnosis and prescription of a physician who received a report of a patient's symptoms via telephone.

A corporate planning specialist in another company said that planning might be done on computers at times when it was not appropriate to do so.

He added that electronic computers were multiplying rapidly in his company, but were often used to regenerate much useless information. This planner and the previously mentioned one both believed that the judgment of individual managers was the key to long-range planning success, and not the use of computers and mathematical models.

OUTLOOK FOR COMPUTER UTILIZATION IN LONG-RANGE PLANNING

In spite of some discouraging experience, operations research techniques and computers were being used by business firms for a wide range of planning applications such as forecasting, evaluating alternatives, and optimizing decisions about future operations. Such applications and the use of computers for collecting planning data will undoubtedly be extended in the future to more companies and to more functional areas within a given company.

Robert S. Weinberg, Director of Analytical Services at the International Business Machines Corporation, stated his view on the value of mathematical techniques for planning in these words: "A good planner is a good professional guesser; models sharpen your ability to guess." He added that "very significant changes will be made (in planning techniques) and it is important to move in this direction, for if the competition becomes systematic (by using models and computers), your chances become very poor." [5]

This view was supported by the comments of other planning specialists, and it provided a sound appraisal of the importance of computer techniques for planning future business activities. More complete and more accurate planning will be possible as computer systems become more versatile, as planning data become more extensive, and as analytical techniques become more elaborate. However, the efforts of staff specialists and operating managers must be integrated to design and utilize these computerized planning systems in order to maximize the value derived from them.

The rapid development of computer service centers in major cities and the availability of standard programs for solving various business management problems will also permit an increasing number of firms to do systematic planning without making a large investment in expensive equipment and personnel.

COMPANY EVALUATIONS OF FORMALIZED PLANNING

In order to determine whether the costs and effort to formalize long-range planning activities were justified, executives and planning specialists in several companies were asked to evaluate their own planning systems. In the remaining section of this chapter, the appraisals of these individuals who were directly involved in long-range planning are reported. Some of the benefits of formal planning, as well as recurring problems, are discussed. Also, a brief appraisal of informal planning systems is included.

BENEFITS OF FORMALIZED LONG-RANGE PLANNING TO A BUSINESS FIRM

A Vice President in a company which had practiced formalized long-range planning for a relatively short period of time made the following evaluation:

> I think we have not been as effective in the past as we could have been if the function had been formalized more quickly than it was. In other words, we were doing a good bit of planning, but it was not being as well followed up and aggressively pushed as I think it can be under our present formal organization structure.

The Director of Corporate Development in another company that established formal planning procedures during the preceding year made a similar appraisal when he said: "We anticipate that the described procedure will be a considerable improvement over the somewhat less formal program of the past."

The value of more formal planning in Allis-Chalmers Manufacturing Company was stated in these words: "Added emphasis by all divisions on operational planning and a greatly strengthened corporate planning program are contributing much in charting profitable courses for the Company to take in the years ahead." [6]

The Vice President of a large chemical company stated that "most divisions which are most profitable are those with the best planning organization and the highest-paid planners."

The impact of formal planning on profits was stressed by one Director of Corporate Planning. He said: "The way to see that the planning system is working is to look at the earnings record." He added: "Without corporate planning, many things that are needed would not get done."

One Vice President said that a major benefit of formalized planning in his company was "the conscientious, systematic examination of problems which resulted from an independent review of plans by an informed, dedicated, and competent group of evaluators—the Corporate Development staff."

An illustration of a tangible benefit which was derived from this type of review was reported by the Director of Corporate Planning in another firm. He said that a proposed mill valued at 15-million dollars was not purchased after long-range projections and a systematic analysis indicated that profits would be reduced if it were obtained.

The benefit of a formal planning staff was stated by another Director of Planning in these words:

> Planners have more time than executives and can take data from all phases of the business, integrate them, and give the executive a better view so he can tell what he doesn't like easily and quickly. Thus, staff planning is a communication device.

When these specific results of formalized long-range planning are analyzed from a corporation point of view, all of them should increase the efficiency and effectiveness of a firm in achieving its objectives. In summary, most of the firms which had formalized their planning procedures expected earnings per unit of invested funds to increase as a result.

INTERNAL COMPANY EVALUATIONS OF PLANNING EFFORTS

The planning efficiency often varied widely between divisions of a given corporation, and some efforts to evaluate internal planning performance were reported. In an electrical equipment manufacturing company, each division under one Group Vice President prepared a five-year plan which was reviewed and graded by this executive. As a result of this action, each manager received a beneficial evaluation of his efforts and also realized that planning was considered an important element of his job.

In another company, the planning staff made informal evaluations of the planning efforts of different operating managers, and favorable comments by the staff, when deserved, would reveal this to the President.

In the International Business Machines Corporation, planning efforts were evaluated by measuring the accomplishments of each division and the corporation, and then comparing these results to previously-set objectives. An important difference was made in evaluating strategic (long-range) plans and operating (short-range) plans. One method used to evaluate strategic plans was to compare them with earlier versions. Another method was to determine the extent to which each planning unit had achieved its "Established Objectives" in each time period. In addition, the feasibility of proposed plans for meeting the challenge of future "Established Key Objectives" was evaluated.

In many other companies, financial results were compared regularly to forecasts which were made in preceding long-range plans. In one company which compared results to forecasts, any significant deviations were embarrassing to the manager who made the forecasts. This evaluation procedure was summarized by a planning specialist in this company as follows: "Department personnel learn to expect that superficial work will bring what they refer to as 'surgical' questions."

The President of another corporation evaluated the efforts of operating managers at the end of the first year of formalized planning by comparing first year results to the predictions in the initial plans of each manager.

When the division managers realized how the President was evaluating their performance, they "got serious" about planning.

Thus, planning efforts in different companies were evaluated by formal reviews, informal appraisals, and periodic comparisons of results with stated objectives or forecasts. Such evaluations should be applied to long-range planning efforts, as to all other functions of business management.

No formal procedures for evaluating the work of planning staffs were reported, but one planner said this was "a touchy area—a political football" in his company.

A study on the cost of planning was being made in another company, for "there is a point of diminishing returns." This is generally true of all functions in business management, and the costs of planning efforts should always be weighed against the expected benefits, even if it is a difficult, subjective task.

In an effort to justify a particular item of cost, the planning staff in one company was evaluating the benefit derived from an expensive external planning service. Other firms had made similar evaluations previously.

APPRAISALS BY COMPANIES WHICH PLANNED INFORMALLY

Some of the companies which had not formalized planning recognized and stated some weaknesses of their informal systems. They mentioned limitations such as poor coordination and the failure of managers to give adequate time and attention to planning due to the press of other current duties.

However, they believed there were some benefits which resulted from an informal planning system. They mentioned advantages such as greater flexibility, swifter competitive moves, better managers due to greater planning responsibility, and better acceptance of plans due to the involvement of managers in planning. Such benefits were not necessarily missing in more formalized systems, and a few of the seven companies which planned informally expected their planning systems to become increasingly formalized.

PROBLEMS IN FORMAL LONG-RANGE PLANNING SYSTEMS

Several problems in formal long-range planning systems were also reported. One planner stated that "top executives don't want to do planning, but don't want to let loose of the reins enough to get adequate help." Thus, it seemed that the executives and/or planners in this firm had not recognized or developed properly their respective roles in long-range planning.

The question of balance and proper relationship between the functions of staff specialists and operating managers was probably not resolved completely in any of the corporations which were investigated. Moreover, it may never be resolved, for activities, personnel, organization structures, and management methods are constantly changing. Nevertheless, the question which should be ever-present can be stated in these terms: How can the efforts of specialized staff planners and analysts be integrated with those of operating managers to maximize the wealth of the stockholders over the long run while fulfilling the social responsibilities of the firm? Even though answers may never be certain, they should continually be sought.

Line-staff conflicts were a major initial problem in one company that had formalized planning in the preceding year. The Vice President of this firm said that "old line men don't understand the concept (of planning) or don't like for anyone, even the Chairman of the Board, to look in on their activities."

Limited cooperation was reported in other companies due to the NIH ("not invented here") factor or due to similar provincial attitudes. The Vice President previously quoted added that "patience is necessary to get acceptance and understanding; once you decide to make an organizational change, it takes a long time to overcome the inertia of the existing structure and procedures." Other planning specialists also reported that the slowness of making changes and becoming more systematic was a major problem in a big company.

Unrealistic projections of financial results for future periods had caused problems in some companies. Earnings performance had not matched expectations in instances due to inaccurate demand forecasts, inflationary cost increases, or product price decreases. Investment decisions proved to be unwise in other situations due to changes in some environmental factor. In an effort to obtain more accurate estimates of future performance, some companies made projections in terms of future expected costs and prices. However, this problem is likely to remain as a major one in long-range planning, for the future is uncertain and forecasts will never be perfect.

One Vice President reported that "decision-making was difficult" in a long-range planning committee. He said that each committee member wanted to bring two or three assistants to the meetings, and the resulting group was too large for effective action. This problem was circumvented by "in-between" meetings and decision-making by five or six of the key members of the regular committee. Incidentally, this was a perfect illustration of Parkinson's Law Number 4.

Poor communication between those who were involved in planning activities frequently led to delays and ineffective action. One planner illustrated this problem when he stated that "a method or procedure developed in Rockefeller Center may not be understood by people in the field." Thus, while frequent interchanges of ideas and discussions of mutual activities were desirable, these types of communication were often not possible due to the widespread geographical dispersion of the operating units in large corporations.

Another problem resulted from transfers of key planning personnel into operating management jobs. Since planners were usually individuals with broad experience and training, they were often selected to fill other important positions. In companies where such transfers had been frequent, it was difficult to maintain continuity in policies and planning activities. One executive reported that his major problem was to find the personnel with the background and ability for planning.

A special type of problem was mentioned by one corporate planner. He believed that sound long-range planning decisions were not made in some instances because of the requirement for quarterly earnings reports from corporations which listed their stock on the major exchanges. The implication was that the short-run goal of producing favorable earnings reports caused some managers to postpone or neglect decisions which would reduce current earnings, even if the prospective long-run results were very favorable. This planner also believed that some managers made decisions which affected current earnings on the basis of expected personal gain from stock trading (due to stock option plans) instead of the long-run objectives of the corporation.

Summary

Formal long-range planning was generally considered to offer significant benefits to business firms, but some problems also existed which reduced planning effectiveness. Therefore, any firm which formalizes long-range planning should be aware of the potential benefits and limitations so it can maximize the value derived from the planning system.

Footnotes for Chapter 3

[1] Such committees in different companies had various names—Long Range Planning, Administrative, Executive, Profit Improvement, Corporate Planning, Growth and Profit Improvement, Management Review, or Board Advisory. In other companies, a group of the highest-level executives reviewed long-range plans or engaged in corporate planning, but were not called committees; they had special names such as The Executive, President's Office, or President's Council.

[2] This company believed that financing for all worthwhile investment proposals could be obtained from internally-generated funds or from external credit, since the earnings performance necessary to provide such funds or to support such credit was always expected.

[3] The plan for an operating unit in one large diversified-products company often included several sub-plans for groups of products which were similar either in nature, in the required production process, or in the type of market served.

[4] *1964 Annual Report—General Electric* (New York: General Electric Company, 1965), p. 22.

[5] Robert S. Weinberg, "A Corporate Model as a Tool for Long-Range Planning," Unpublished proceedings of the Eighth Annual Symposium on Planning, April 26, 1965, New York, N. Y. (Sponsored by The Institute of Management Sciences, College on Planning).

[6] *Allis-Chalmers Annual Report—1964* (West Allis, Wisconsin: Allis-Chalmers Manufacturing Company, 1965), p. 7.

Chapter 4

The Long-Range Planning System at International Minerals and Chemical Corporation

NATURE OF THE COMPANY

International Minerals and Chemical Corporation (IMC), the world's largest privately-owned producer of fertilizer materials, mines phosphate rock and potash and produces nitrogen in a jointly-owned ammonia plant. These three basic ingredients of fertilizer are sold separately in domestic and international markets, and are also mixed and sold as ready-to-use plant food. IMC also markets a line of more than 80 diversified products, including industrial chemicals and minerals, animal feed ingredients, pesticides, and a food flavor enhancer. The foundry, steel, ceramics, glass, and oil well-drilling industries are served by the company, as well as agricultural and consumer markets.

Over 200 mines, plants, and sales offices are located in many different parts of the United States and in a few foreign countries. The company has grown very rapidly in recent years, with a sales volume in fiscal year 1965 (263-million dollars) which more than doubled the volume in fiscal year 1960. IMC ranks near the middle of the 500 largest United States corporations on the basis of sales.

THE ORGANIZATION FOR LONG-RANGE PLANNING

IMC had one of the most highly formalized planning systems of any of the companies studied. A Corporate Planning and Development Division with approximately 80 members was responsible for important long-range planning activities. Approximately two-thirds of this staff were professional employees, and the remaining one-third were clerical workers. This Division served as a corporate staff unit to coordinate planning by the company's operating units and to perform special services and investigations.

Vice President Gordon O. Pehrson was in charge of the Planning and Development Division, which had an annual budget in excess of 1-million dollars. The number of planners and operations research specialists in IMC was believed to be greater per unit of sales than in any other corporation in the United States.

The formally stated functions of the Planning and Development Division were:

1. to provide environmental "intelligence" and to measure the impact of environmental factors on the company,
2. to develop strategic plans which were responsive to existing challenges,
3. to determine optimum resource allocation,
4. to seek and develop opportunities in major new ventures, and
5. to monitor operating performance and precipitate responsive decision making.

The five units of this Division were called—Market Research, Strategic (Program) Planning, Venture Development, Information Systems, and Organization Planning.

The Market Research staff was responsible for:

1. providing basic economic and political "intelligence,"
2. providing industry and competitor "intelligence,"
3. identifying and measuring new opportunities and threats to the company,

4. evaluating and assembling information for corporate and divisional use, and
5. providing supporting market facts for proposed new ventures.

The Strategic (Program) Planning group was responsible for developing corporate-level strategies and formal planning procedures, and for coordinating all planning efforts. The members of this planning unit prepared and issued instructions and timetables for long-range planning which was done by each operating unit and functional staff. Later, they received and reviewed written plans which were submitted by the various operating and staff units in the company. They also formulated criteria for strategic planning which were published and distributed to operating managers in "program-package" guides, and held strategic planning meetings to counsel and assist in the synthesis of "market-mission" strategies. In addition, this unit helped determine project priorities and optimum resource allocation. They also brought major challenges or issues to the attention of top management, and recommended appropriate action responses.

Donald J. Smalter, Director of Strategic Planning, was in charge of this group and served as the key planning coordinator in the company. He and Robert A. Mocella, Corporate Planner, provided most of the data in this chapter on planning procedures, responsibility assignments, and strategic planning.

The Venture Development group was responsible for identifying and screening new business opportunities. They also analyzed and developed those which led to new ventures for fulfilling strategic company goals. This staff appraised and implemented acquisitions and evaluated capital plans. They developed programming for approved major projects and initiated action on such projects. In addition, they planned and implemented tests and commercialization of major new products.

The Information Systems group consisted of two sections—Management Sciences and Data Processing. The Management Sciences unit included specialists on operations research techniques and computer programming. They conducted optimization studies on new and existing "systems," analyzed strategic alternatives, and determined the best courses of action mathematically. They also provided analytical problem-solving services to other company units for functions such as mine planning, logistic analysis, and venture analysis.

The Data Processing section was responsible for operating and improving the information systems of the corporation. They were especially concerned with performance reporting for various operating units and "missions" of the company, and prepared reports on results which could be readily assimilated by top management. They also programmed and managed a data-processing control system.

The fifth unit of the Corporate Planning and Development Division was the Organization Planning group. The members of this unit developed personnel policies and organization structures, and were also engaged in long-range manpower planning. A computerized personnel classification system was used in IMC to locate qualified members of the organization to fill management jobs.

In addition to the corporate planning groups, there were also staff planners who reported to the operating managers throughout the company, even at mines and plants. "Operations research" specialists were also assigned to the larger installations, and they worked closely with the planner in each organizational unit. There were approximately ten planners in IMC in operating units below the divisional level. At the divisional level, there were five administrative managers who coordinated planning activities in each of the five major operating divisions. These divisional planners also provided liaison between the corporate planning staff and the operating units. In the future, the divisional planning staffs may be expanded in IMC.

THE CONCEPT OF STRATEGIC PLANNING

Strategy Defined

"Strategy" was the watchword for long-range planning by managers in IMC. It was defined in written form as follows to serve as an everpresent guide: "How best to deploy limited resources in order to maximize profits—in the changing environment, against competition, in pursuit of goals." Thus, "strategy" was the basic approach or broad plan of action used to maximize the wealth of the IMC stockholders, while providing economic goods to satisfy human wants in a competitive and everchanging environment.

Alternative Business Strategies

The resources of a going manufacturing and mining firm such as IMC include: money, real estate (including mineral deposits), plants and equipment, production systems and technology, material and product stocks, marketing systems, research and development results and capabilities, loyal employees, an existing organization, and the good will of external groups and individuals. The economic goods to be produced in the future to achieve the basic profit goal and other social goals may be (1) existing (currently-produced) products, or (2) new products. Also, the economic wants to be satisfied may be classified as (1) those in existing markets (those the company now serves), or (2) those in new markets.

Therefore, the basic framework for strategic planning in IMC, as well as in other progressive companies, was to consider the future need for existing products in existing and new markets, and also to consider the future need for new products in existing and new markets. This simple matrix offers four fundamental strategies for planning future activities in any business firm:

Strategy No. 1—provide existing products to existing markets (current market penetration may be maintained, increased, or decreased),

Strategy No. 2—provide existing products to new markets (develop markets),

Strategy No. 3—provide new products to existing markets (develop products),

Strategy No. 4—provide new products to new markets (develop products and markets).

To determine the most desirable strategy or strategies from among these alternatives, three fundamental types of analysis should be made. First, product needs in existing and potential markets at future points in time should be predicted. Next, the resources which a firm possesses or can obtain for satisfying these projected product (or service) needs should be analyzed. The nature, extent, and mixture of resources should be evaluated in relation to those of existing and potential competitors. Finally, the profitability and long-run benefits of alternative uses of resources should be estimated. This basic approach to long-range planning was followed in IMC, where a primary objective was to develop a "mix" of company "growth" strategies.

PLANS REQUIRED FOR ALTERNATIVE STRATEGIES

A given company may adopt one or more of the basic market-product strategies. When Strategy No. 1 is followed, "operations plans" should be formulated for future periods of times to indicate how the company's resources will be utilized. In IMC, the "operations plans" included five sub-plans for major functional activities—technical support, production, marketing-sales, financial, and administrative.

When Strategy No. 2 or No. 3 is adopted, "development plans" must be formulated to implement either strategy. At IMC, the "development plan" included sub-plans for raw materials, acquisitions, growth through research and development, and projects. A "divestment plan" may also grow out of either Strategy No. 1, 2, or 3.

When Strategy No. 4 is adopted, a special type of "development plan" is formulated. It was called a "diversification plan" in IMC, and included sub-plans for acquisitions or mergers and for research and development.

This entire system of strategic plans, as diagrammed in chart form by the IMC planning staff, is reproduced in Figure 1. It indicates how the

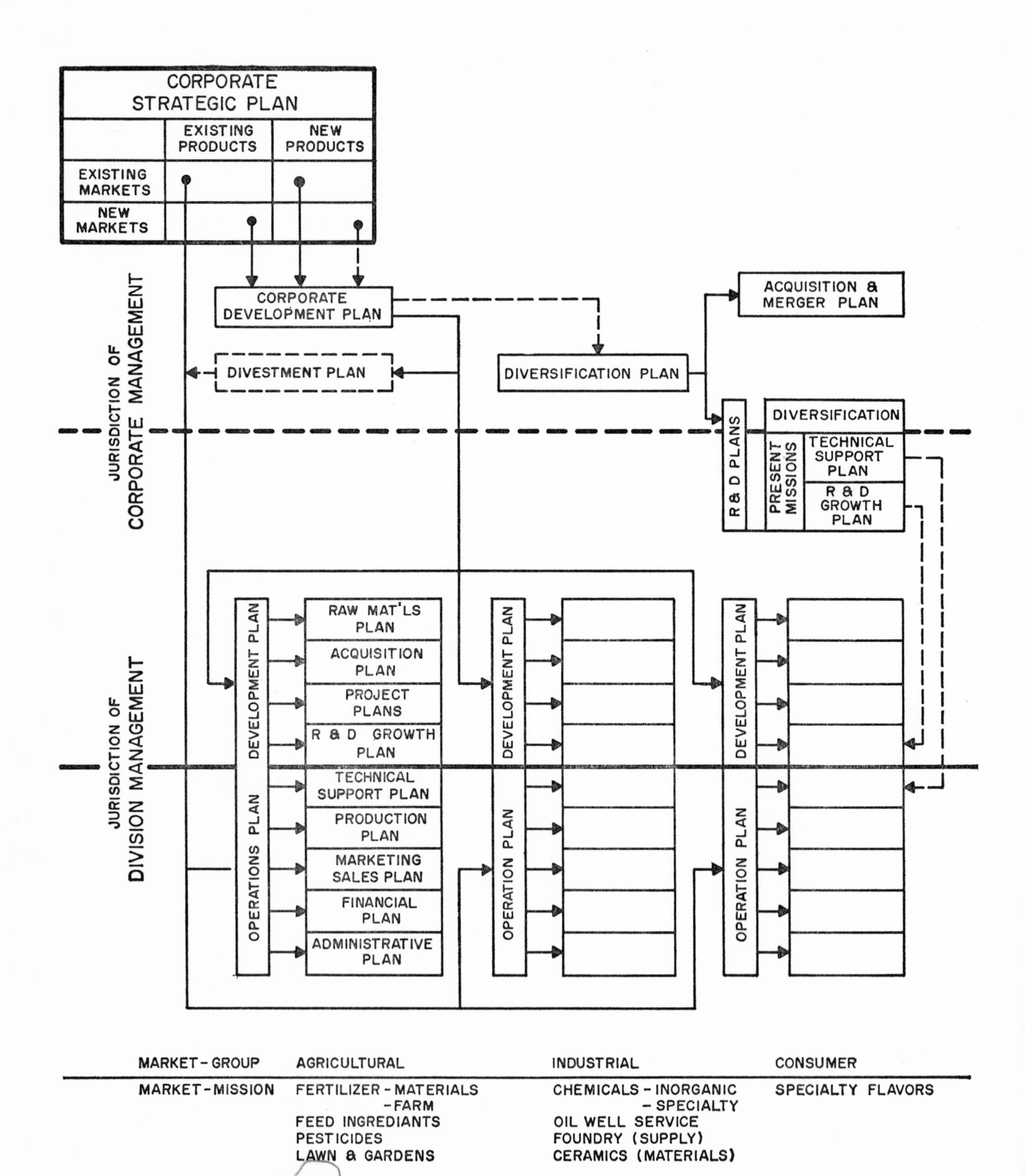

Figure 1: System of Strategic Plans in International Minerals and Chemical Corporation

various plans and sub-plans grew out of the four basic market-product strategy alternatives. The division of responsibility for plan formation between divisional and corporate management is also shown in Figure 1. The IMC division managers and planners developed "operations plans" and worked with the corporate planning staff and top management on division "development plans," while the corporate planners and executives formulated corporate "development plans" and some derivative plans.

The "operations" and "development" plans in IMC were prepared for each of several "market-missions." Since the functional task or "mission" of a business organization is to provide specific goods to specific markets, a "market-mission" plan in IMC pertained to making and selling a particular line of products to a particular market. For example, "market-missions" pertained to fertilizer materials, inorganic chemicals, specialty flavors, and many other product groups. The plans for each "market-mission" were then combined into plans for one of three "market-groups"—agricultural, industrial, or consumer. This organization of plans by market missions and groups is also indicated in Figure 1.

The system of strategic planning in IMC was viewed alternatively as a three-dimensional matrix where (1) various types of resources were allocated among (2) various "market-missions" (and broader "market-groups") for (3) each of several time periods in the future. Managers in IMC were admonished when they developed long-range plans to balance the allocation of resources for selected market purposes in proper dimensions of time. They were expected to do their best, but were reminded that complete program balance was difficult to attain.

THE PROCESS OF STRATEGIC PLANNING BY MISSIONS

CORPORATE STRATEGY DEVELOPMENT

Strategic planning by missions must begin by formulation of a corporate strategy. This process involved four major steps in IMC, and each step included several analytical procedures.

First, existing missions and commitments of resources were reviewed and summarized. An analysis was made of the position of the company with respect to each mission, and the future business environment was forecast. Then goals and strategies for the future were proposed, and company strengths and weaknesses were specified.

The second step was an assessment of additional opportunities. The potential for growth in the existing business was determined, and new potentially profitable opportunities were identified. The alternatives of internally-generated growth or external acquisitions were analyzed in view of existing financial constraints and other important factors.

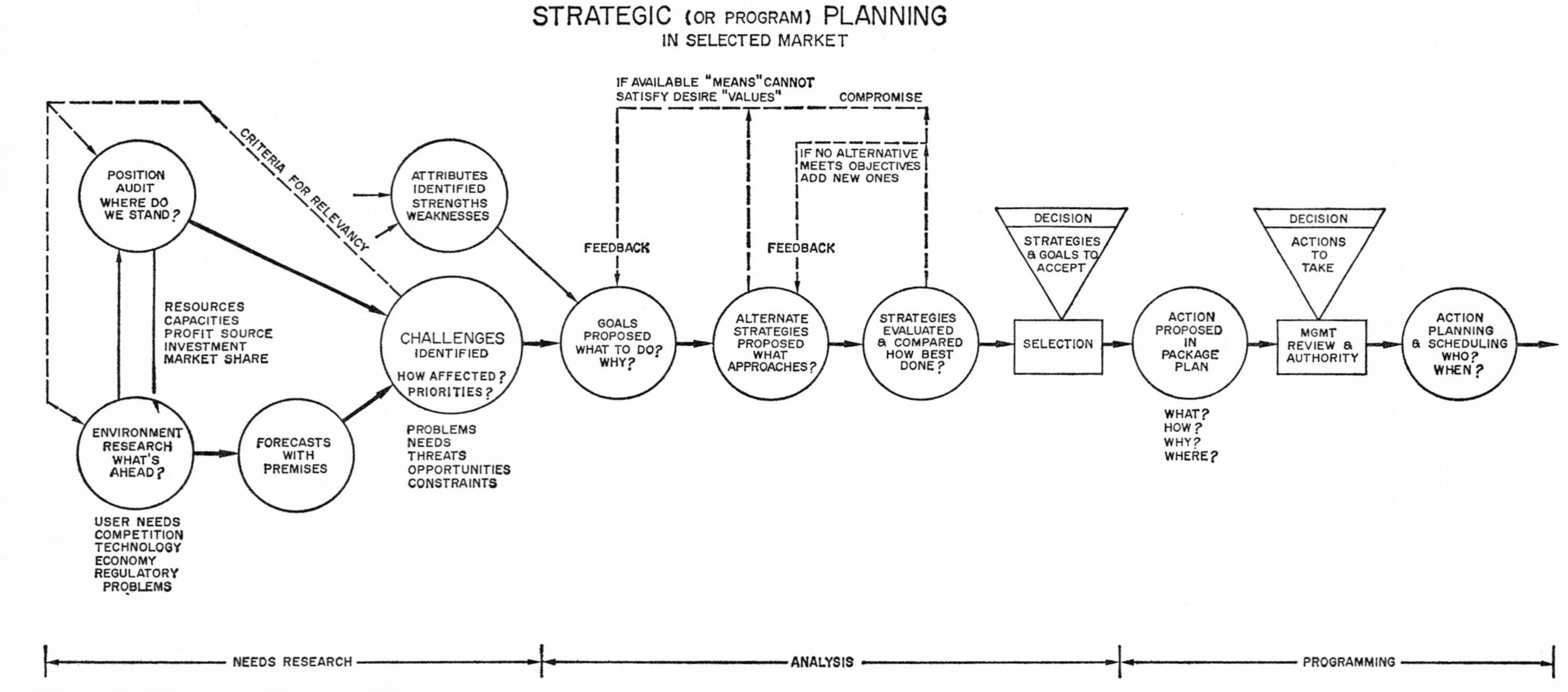

Figure 2: Elements of Strategic Planning in International Minerals and Chemical Corporation

The third step was to synthesize an overall growth strategy. A "philosophy of growth" was clearly defined and accepted in terms of objectives and goals. The future importance of diversification was defined, and acquisition criteria were specified.

The final step was to resolve specific mission strategies, and to set goals for each new mission.

STEPS IN STRATEGIC MISSION PLANNING

The sequential steps of strategic planning in IMC for a specific "market-mission" are shown in schematic form in Figure 2. An initial assessment of the company's current position in the selected market was made, and existing challenges were identified and assigned a priority. Then specific goals were proposed and alternative strategies were outlined and evaluated. The most promising ones were expanded into concrete program proposals which were reviewed by top management. After approval, a given program was planned in much greater detail for efficient implementation.

Thus, "strategic planning" in IMC included performance evaluation, environmental forecasting, needs research, goal-setting, strategy formulation and selection, and programming. All long-range planning in the company was based on strategic considerations, instead of merely extending current activities into the future. "Strategy" was used in a more restricted sense by other companies, but at IMC, it was continually stressed and broadly applied. As a reflection of this emphasis, the position of "Director of Strategic Planning" in IMC was believed to be unique among business corporations.

DYNAMIC NATURE OF LONG-RANGE PLANNING

The dynamic nature of long-range planning was clearly portrayed in the process of strategic planning at IMC. Goals were set, strategies were formulated, and programs were planned as in the customary static view of the planning process. However, each of these steps was not independent and final. When the time dimension was added and the impact of one goal, strategy, or program on other elements of planning were considered, and when a balance was sought in resource allocation, the feedback often required a change in a preceding step. Goals, strategies, or specific programs might be revised, for all were interrelated. The good or bad results of past planning which were reflected in current performance and the ever-changing conditions in the business environment also caused planning to be dynamic in nature.

If corporate long-range planning is to be effective, it must be a continual process of obtaining feedback about financial performance and research results, and then synthesizing these data with fresh inputs on environmental changes and executive judgments. The system of "strategic planning" in IMC, with its regular sequence of planning steps, its information inputs, and its formal organization with clearly-defined functional responsibilities, seemed to provide the mechanism for effective forward planning.

PLANNING PROCEDURES

The formal planning cycle in IMC required a 12-month period for completion, and then it was repeated. The procedures followed during this cycle included three major steps, as shown in sequence with the approximate time periods indicated for each step:

1. Planning (July–November)
   a) needs and opportunities were identified and studied, and
   b) the strategy framework was resolved;
2. Programming (October–March)
   a) program goals were formulated, development projects were specified, and
   b) five-year plans were assembled and reviewed;
3. Budgeting or Annual Profit Planning (March–June)
   a) the budget, a one year slice of five-year plans, was prepared.

Each of the five basic activities performed during this planning cycle is described in the following sections.

NEEDS RESEARCH

The function of "needs research" was a continual one for the corporate planning staff and for other full time planning personnel in IMC. Each group in the Corporate Planning and Development Division was assigned a specific role in "needs research." The Market Research and Information Systems groups prepared various forecasts for each major operating unit in the company early in the planning cycle, while other groups in the Division were engaged in activities to identify needs and opportunities.

The primary reason for assigning these activities to the corporate planning staff members was that they possessed the necessary specialized skills and time to perform this basic planning role. Persons with primary responsibility for operational activities generally did not have the necessary time, skills, or orientation for such work. However, operating managers were always alert for specific needs and opportunities.

MISSION STRATEGY RESOLUTION

The next activity in the planning cycle was to resolve the strategy framework for each major operating unit. Meetings were scheduled separately for each unit, and divisional personnel presented strategy proposals for each of several "missions." In addition to the operating personnel, staff specialists from finance, research and development, corporate planning, and possibly mining and exploration would attend these meetings. A Vice President, a project director, or a member of the corporate planning staff would preside, and each proposed mission program was reviewed and discussed for three hours or more.

Since missions pertained to product groupings and the company was organized on a product-line basis, most missions pertained to only one division. For example, the Plant Food Division or Industrial Minerals Division was fully responsible for certain missions. However, other missions such as "industrial chemicals" or "animal health" cut across two or more divisions. In this case, a project director developed and presented a mission strategy.

Each proposed mission strategy included a review of the available strategies for each functional area of activity—marketing, distribution, production, financial-administrative, and research-development. For example, available market strategies might be either to increase product usage, to increase IMC's share of the market, or to expand services to customers. Available financial strategies might be either to acquire outside companies, to participate in joint ventures, or to dispose of unwanted assets.

After reviewing possibilities, some of the available strategies for each functional area were proposed for adoption, and the degree of emphasis (primary or secondary) or priority (high, medium, or low) was specified for each strategy. Then, the strategic response, or broad action plans, were outlined. Each mission strategy was resolved at these committee meetings in keeping with broader corporate strategy and goals.

PROGRAM GOAL FORMULATION

Program goals were then formulated in more specific terms as broad action plans were expanded into detailed methods of implementation. A "program-package" for each mission was assembled which provided the foundation of the five-year plans. An outline or planning checklist which IMC used for developing a mission "program-package" is reproduced in Table 4. This outline was expanded into a four-page set of fundamental questions in a planning manual to serve as a guide and framework for mission planning by managers and staff specialists.

PREPARATION OF FIVE-YEAR PLANS

To initiate formal plan preparation, a "call letter" was sent from the Corporate Planning and Development Division to the Vice President in charge of each major operating unit in the company. This letter, distributed in August, contained a request for the preparation and submission of five-year plans.

Instructions for plan preparation were also provided at this time. They contained a planning time schedule and suggested the formats and pro-

Table 4: An Outline of Mission Plans in International Minerals and Chemical Corporation

CHARTER
- Scope/Purpose/Objectives
- Product-Line Concept
  - Unique "values" offered
  - Proprietary Directions
  - New-Frontier Aims

POSITION (Present & Future)
- Industry Structure & Character
- Profit Sources
- Product Life-Cycle Status
- Market Share & Area
- Capacity Utilization, etc.

ATTRIBUTES (OR CAPABILITIES)
- Strengths
- Weaknesses

ENVIRONMENT (Present & Future)
- Market Demand Outlook
- Competition and Price
- Distribution Channels
- Changing Technology
- Economy Trends
- Regulatory Constraints
- Community Constraints

IMPACT ON IMC
- Problems & Needs
- Threats
- Opportunities

} Priorities in Response?

MOMENTUM -- Present Operations
- Prospects/Goals
- Premises
- P&L Summary

BUSINESS DEVELOPMENT ACTION-PROGRAMS
- Response to Attributes
- Response to Challenges

} How?
- Alternatives Considered/Selected
- Resource "Handling"
  - Capital Projects
  - Geographical Expansion
  - Raw Material Needs
  - Services & Merchandising
  - Acquisition Goals
  - Financial Demands

TECHNICAL PROGRAM
- Support
  - Cost reduction
  - Product improvement
  - Sales service
  - Market application development
- Innovative

ORGANIZATION -- Needs & Plans

GOALS
- Sales
- Profits

} Performance (& Comparison w/others)

QUESTIONS: Completeness?.. Soundness?.. How Execute?

cedures to be followed in order to insure adequate uniformity among divisional plans. A sample format of a complete five-year plan (approximately 75 pages) was also sent to the operating units to illustrate methods for presenting action plans. However, each division was permitted to digress somewhat from the standard format and to utilize its own unique style.

In the 1964-1965 planning cycle, a request and a sample format for five-year action programs and cost projections were also sent to all corporate staff units in IMC for the first time. The reason for this action was stated in a cover letter as follows: "The interdependence of the business missions and the corporate (staff) functions needs to be more clearly related through mutually consistent objectives." In two preceding planning cycles, only the operating or "line" units were asked to prepare long-range plans.

Five-year plans were prepared by each operating unit which included projections of sales, revenues, costs, net income, and capital expenditures. Also, performance projections were made in terms of net profit/sales, net profit/fixed assets, and net profit/investment. These projections were ratios of dollar values, and "investment" was defined as the sum of fixed asset value, non-capital project expenses, and working capital needs (as related primarily to projected sales). Staff plans included projections of costs only, since these units did not produce revenues. Detailed work plans were also included in five-year plans for potential acquisitions, proposed production facilities, and other action programs.

After assembly at different levels in the organization, the five-year plans were sent to the Corporate Planning and Development Division for review by the various specialized staff groups. Any questions or problems pertaining to the plans were resolved, and they were sent to the top executives for review and approval. Finally, a consolidated, condensed plan was presented to the Board of Directors.

ANNUAL PLAN PREPARATION

The final step in the planning cycle was the preparation of an "annual profit plan" for the coming year. This plan consisted primarily of operating budgets and capital investment programs. Such plans were expected to correspond closely to those for the first year in the five-year plans, but they were more specific. For example, only the capital investment projects which were expected to cost over $50,000 were detailed in the five-year plans, while those estimated to cost over $15,000 were detailed in the annual plans.

OPERATIONS RESEARCH IN LONG-RANGE PLANNING

Operations research techniques and electronic computers played an important role in long-range planning at IMC. Specific applications had been made in the past, and new techniques and areas of utilization were continually being developed and evaluated. Four specific uses of operations research in planning were described by members of the Corporate Planning and Development Division. These applications pertained to: (1) plant location, (2) debt maximization, (3) product distribution, and (4) ocean transportation.

PLANT LOCATION

Donald J. Smalter, Director of Strategic Planning, described how a mathematical model used by oil companies to optimize service station locations was adapted and used to optimize the location of mineral and fertilizer processing plants in various market areas.

Many quantifiable variables which affected operating and distribution costs were incorporated into the model. These variables pertained to all buyers and sellers of the product to be produced in the new plant. They included: the location of each market area; the projected sales volume for each buyer in future periods of time (up to five years); the location, distribution costs, and operating costs of each competitive supplier; the share of the market currently held by each supplier; and the potential alternative actions by competitors (including a probability of occurrence for each such action).

Before the model was used to solve the specific problem of selecting the best geographical locations for new plants, several of the best potential locations were designated by screening many possible ones on the basis of specific selection criteria. Then each of these "better" locations was tested for profitability in the model, using computer calculations.

In this manner, it was possible to select the "best" locations, or those where the long-run profit potential was maximized and the probability of harmful competition was minimized. Changes in prices which might result from competitor's actions were also estimated and used in the computations. The production capacity of each plant and the sequence for constructing particular plants were also optimized in view of the pattern of expected future demand, existing supply sources, available funds, and other critical factors.

After the first plant was built, the profitability tests were repeated with the basic mathematical model for the remaining "best" locations. However, more recent data on the volumes and locations of potential supplies and demands for the product under study were used. Also, any action taken by a competitor in the interim was included. This reexamination was made to determine if locations or the building sequence should be revised in order to maximize profitability.

Mr. Smalter pointed out that a serious limitation of most market research efforts, including even computerized programs of recent years, had been the failure to consider probable actions of competitors. When this important variable was ignored, otherwise reliable estimates of potential markets often led to overexpansion. The resulting excess capacity and fixed costs increased production costs per unit of product, thereby reducing profit margins and rates of return on investments.

The refinement used by IMC to predict competitor's actions and assign probabilities to them seemed to be a significant improvement in long-range planning techniques.

DEBT-MAXIMIZATION

Mr. Smalter also stated that studies were being made at IMC to determine the maximum level of debt, in a given investment of debt and equity capital, which could be incurred while maintaining an acceptable degree of risk. Maximizing debt within certain risk constraints is a desirable goal for a "growth" company with investment opportunities which require funds in excess of the amount generated internally. Also, the generally lower cost of debt capital and the tax saving from interest deductions enables "financial leverage" to boost earnings per share of common stock. However, as financial or operating leverage increases, the probability of incurring a loss also increases. Thus, the optimum debt level, or that which leads to maximum long-run profits, is the desired goal.

This problem of optimizing the debt level revolves about (1) the estimation of various possible levels of monetary profit or loss if each of various "debt to equity" ratios exist in the company's financial structure, and (2) the estimation of a probability of occurrence for each possible loss.

To solve this problem in IMC, a mathematical model was being developed to include all significant variables which affected net income, such as sales volume, unit prices, and unit costs. Several possible values for each of the variables in the model were to be assumed for future periods of time, and a probability of occurrence assigned to each value. Then alternative solutions could be obtained in units of net profit or loss, with corresponding probabilities of occurrence, by making computer calculations.

This approach should provide a systematic method of optimizing the fraction of debt in the company's financial structure. It could also be used to simulate the outcome of alternative investment strategies, and appeared to be a useful new technique for long-range planning. If estimates are made carefully from market research and other input data, decisions on the debt level to be accepted should certainly be more reliable than if based on some traditional criteria.

The attitudes of executives, such as an undue fear or disdain for debt, or the opposite view of "nothing ventured—nothing gained," sometimes have a decisive effect on the debt level in United States corporations. Other arbitrary criteria, such as the availability of debt or equity funds, are often used. However, the firm that seeks to optimize its debt level, by using a systematic approach such as the one which IMC was developing, is likely to earn the highest rate of return on the stockholder's equity over an extended period of time.

PRODUCT DISTRIBUTION

Dr. Sidney Singer, Manager of the Management Sciences section, described two specific applications of linear programming to operational problems in IMC which have significant implications for long-range planning. One of these was to ascertain the optimal distribution pattern of fertilizer raw materials (potash or phosphate rock) throughout the world. This problem was of the "general transportation" type, which has been stated precisely as follows:

> A homogenous product is to be shipped in the amounts $a_1, a_2, \ldots, a_m$, respectively, from each of m shipping origins and received in amounts $b_1, b_2, \ldots, b_n$, respectively, by each of n shipping destinations. The cost of shipping a unit amount from the i'th origin to the j'th destination is c_{ij} and is known for all combinations (i, j). The problem is to determine the amounts x_{ij} to be shipped over all routes (i, j) so as to minimize the total cost of transportation.[1]

Instead of limiting the problem to their own current sources of supply and markets (as for short-run optimization of distribution routes), IMC included the locations of all current suppliers of the product under consideration and all points of current demand (buyers). In addition, potential points of supply and demand were predicted for several years in the future and included for certain analyses.

The basic economic choice was to determine how a rational allocation would take place if the criterion was lowest cost per unit of product. The distribution costs were very important in this problem, but production costs were also included, since they often varied between supply points. Even though "cost per unit" was the best criterion, it was recognized that other economic or political factors might be decisive.

This model was used by IMC to evaluate the impact of:

1. an actual or projected change in production costs,
2. an actual or projected change in distribution costs,
3. an actual or potential new source of supply, or
4. an actual or potential new point of demand.

In addition, it was used to evaluate relative "delivered costs" of suppliers for the purpose of making judgments on pricing. The model was also useful for market research and development, since market penetration was often determined by the relative cost advantage of one supplier among competitors. Investment opportunities at potential supply locations could be evaluated, and the impact and likelihood of alternative actions by competitors could be predicted.

OCEAN TRANSPORTATION

Dr. Singer also reviewed another application of linear programming to long-range planning which was closely related to the preceding distribution problem. It pertained to the selection of the lowest-cost shipping arrangement for transporting fertilizer raw materials across the ocean from IMC's present supply sources to various points of demand. It was really an extension of the transportation problem in the area of distribution costs.

Three alternative methods existed to provide the needed shipping services:

1. spot chartering of ships (like hiring a taxi),
2. time chartering of ships, and
3. owning some or all of the required number of ships.

The basic consideration was to determine the optimal economic combination of spot-chartering, time-chartering, and fleet ownership in order to minimize distribution costs.

The situation which led to this application of operations research to long-range planning has been summarized as follows:

> At present, transportation costs average $8 a ton on the four million tons of fertilizer materials that IMC ships overseas annually. This is enough tonnage to keep busy a fleet of thirty 15,000-ton vessels the year around—the same number of ships as are in the fleet of the American President Lines. Within a decade the tonnage hauled by IMC is expected to double; the company expects to be shipping an astonishing one out of every 100 to 150 tons of cargo shipped by all the countries of the world. When it is realized that transportation costs in time of shipping shortage can range as high as *four* times the most efficient cost of production, one grasps the opportunity for ingenious economizing.[2]

In order to determine the cheapest shipping method over an extended period of time, it was necessary for the operations research specialists in IMC to develop the basic information needed for decision making. Appropriate shipping cost data were not readily available, so they had to learn what cost elements existed in operating a shipping service, and then determine composite costs from published data or estimates of element cost values.

Optimal routing patterns were determined in IMC by using the general linear program and computer calculations. In addition, comparative costs of alternative shipping methods were developed and the alternatives were evaluated as part of the broader distribution problem. The decision was made to get into the ocean shipping business as a result of this application of operations research.

To illustrate the importance and benefit of efforts to reduce shipping costs, an account of one action follows:

> Last year IMC arranged a long-term charter on a converted T-2 tanker that regularly hauls rice between California and Puerto Rico. On the return leg the boat carries phosphate from Tampa to the West Coast at a rate of $2 a ton less than the rail charge paid by Idaho phosphate producers, who have had the western markets all to themselves for a long time. At a stroke, IMC picked up more than one-third of the more than 300,000-ton-a-year California phosphate market.[3]

As a result of this type of systematic analysis and planning, plus the willingness to base decisions on economics instead of tradition, IMC was moving into the shipping business. Many decisions had to be made, such as those pertaining to the procurement of ships, financing, operating policies and procedures, personnel, maintenance, and timing. Such decisions are an integral part of long-range planning for future business activities, and the use of operations research techniques in making them can lead to better decisions and greater profitability. The personnel at IMC certainly believed this to be true, and their record supported their confidence.

IMPLEMENTATION OF OPERATIONS RESEARCH IN PLANNING

Dr. Singer believed that the role of operations research personnel and techniques was to provide support for long-range planning, in addition to performing shorter-range operational planning. He also stressed the importance of implementation in any operations research study. In IMC, this often involved the training and guidance of operating personnel until they could use a new technique. Such techniques then became inputs to the process of longer-term planning, which was viewed in IMC as the responsibility of the "line" or operating units, as well as that of the corporate-level staff.

These ultimate users of operations research must ask questions, Dr. Singer noted, so that they relate the value of more accurate outputs to the costs of obtaining them. Unjustified costs may result if the economics involved are not considered. Another limitation in applying operations research techniques, according to Dr. Singer, was "the tendency of some to view situations which require a probabilistic analysis from a fixed or deterministic standpoint, due to an inability to accept and/or comprehend a probabilistic approach." However, such techniques can become valuable tools for long-range planning if limitations are recognized and minimized, and if their costs are justified.

EVALUATION OF FORMAL LONG-RANGE PLANNING

Benefits of Formal Long-Range Planning

The Corporate Planning and Development Division in IMC, after only a few years of existence, offered a wide range of specialized services to operating managers and top executives. These services were widely sought throughout the organization, in contrast to the early days when the division was "struggling for acceptance." This fact spoke favorably of the value and success of the formalized long-range planning function.

One of the most significant changes in IMC in recent years was a sharp rise in profits and rate of growth. Formalized planning and development deserved a significant share of the credit for this performance, according to members of the organization. Other reported benefits which may have been reflected in profits were improved communications, better coordination of activities, and a more thorough analysis of all aspects of business management and company activities.

Limitations of Formal Long-Range Planning

The planning process at IMC was not without limitations, for the planning staff reported that procedures sometimes looked better on paper than when efforts were made to put them into effect. Some inefficiency and instances of failure to follow time schedules or specified planning sequences were evident to those intimately involved in long-range planning. The need for more active involvement of some managers in planning was also expressed. Another problem was created because some managers presented too many alternative projects instead of screening them and presenting only the very best.

There is also the potential problem in any large centralized planning staff that planners become too possessive toward plans or too rigid in their views of the best planning procedures. The potential for internal growth to the point where benefits do not justify costs is also present in a planning staff, as in any unit of an organization. However, these problems were not observed in IMC, and adequate "organizational" emphasis seemed to be given to the development and execution of plans.

General Appraisal

In spite of a few problems which were common to all business firms, the planning system in IMC seemed to be very effective, and the organization for planning was very broad and highly integrated. Active participation of operating managers in planning was realized in a relatively short time period, and these managers also learned to utilize specialized staff planning services.

On the basis of discussions with company personnel and other observations, the formalization of long-range planning in IMC was a very beneficial change. The success of the planning system may be attributed to the active support of executives, to the diligent efforts of competent staff specialists, and to the willingness of operating managers to make changes and to utilize new techniques.

Footnotes for Chapter 4

[1] Saul I. Gass, *Linear Programming Methods and Applications* (2d ed.; New York: McGraw-Hill Book Co., Inc., 1964), p. 193.

[2] Richard J. Whalen, "I. M. C.: The Miner Who Shook the Fertilizer Market," *Fortune,* LXXI, No. 3 (March, 1965), 150.

[3] *Ibid.*

Chapter 5

Decentralized Long-Range Planning in Motorola Inc.

The long-range planning system in Motorola Inc. is described and analyzed in this chapter. The Motorola system of decentralized planning provides a sharp contrast to the more centralized planning system of the International Minerals and Chemical Corporation which is described in the preceding chapter.

The factual material presented in this chapter was provided by John T. Hickey, Vice President, Planning and former Director of Long-Range Planning. Mr. Hickey played a major role in helping Robert W. Galvin, Chairman of the Board of Directors and former President, to introduce formalized planning in the corporation.

NATURE AND ORGANIZATION OF THE COMPANY

Motorola is a major producer of diverse electronics products, and is engaged in extensive domestic and international marketing activities. The company has six fully-integrated divisions, as follows: Consumer Products Division, Automobile Products Division, Communications Division, Control Systems Division, Semiconductor Products Division, and Military Electronics Division. Each of these major divisions is under the direction of a General Manager, and in most units, the division head is also a Vice President. The company is decentralized to a significant degree, and each General Manager has broad functional responsibility and authority.

THE ORGANIZATION FOR LONG-RANGE PLANNING

Long-range planning was formalized in Motorola in 1962, and Mr. Hickey was appointed Director of Long-Range Planning. He had the major staff responsibility for corporate planning and reported to Mr. Galvin, who was President at that time. He had no planning staff, except for secretarial help, because his primary task was to guide operating managers in their planning activities and to motivate them to get planning done. The functions of this planning director were to develop formal planning procedures, to coordinate divisional planning, to review plans, and to serve as a catalyst for planning throughout the company. He stated that his job was "not to plan, but to provide the occasion, the motivation, some assistance, and defined requirements to the line managers whose responsibilities include a large measure of planning." He spent approximately 75 per cent of his time on long-range planning activities.

Most of Motorola's divisions had a staff member who was responsible for preparing long-range plans. In one division, a Director of Planning performed this function. He reported to the General Manager of the division and had only minimal functional responsibility to the Director of Long-Range Planning. In other divisions, a marketing or market research specialist, or the controller, was responsible for preparing long-range plans. The staff planner in every division served in a coordinating role, with the responsibility for planning remaining with the general managers.

PHILOSOPHY OF PLANNING

Motorola's stated purpose was "growth," with the focus on profitable growth. Profit was considered the primary business objective—one that transcended all others—for neither growth nor the responsibilities to various groups in society could be fulfilled unless the business was profitable. Thus, the crucial measures of effective management in the company were profit, profit growth, and return on investment.

Planning was considered essential for achieving satisfactory performance. Formalized long-range planning was defined as "the orderly process by which management rationally decides both the amount of growth it intends the business to achieve and the product and market directions in which it expects to achieve this growth." Such planning "is based on realistic appraisal of the prospects for the outside environment, and a sound evaluation of the company's present strengths and weaknesses; it also includes tactics (specific plans) for pursuing the intended growth in the intended directions."

Long-range planning or forward planning was viewed in Motorola as an inherent function of management. It was considered to be a basic task of the line managers, and one that could not properly be delegated to staff personnel. The proper role of the staff was "to encourage, facilitate, and coordinate adequate planning by the line."

The formality of writing things down was considered essential for effective planning, due to the belief that "if you can't write it down, you haven't thought it out." Other stated advantages of written plans were to prevent misunderstanding, to improve communications, and to prevent rationalization of changes in "direction." However, the preparation of a "plan" was not the important goal. The process of planning and the conversion of plans into action by individuals were considered the vital activities. The whole purpose of planning in Motorola was to help managers change "directions."

The four basic market-product strategies which are available to any business firm were considered carefully by Motorola in choosing its business strategy. These strategies were introduced and explained in chapter 4 and are illustrated in matrix form in Figure 3. Strategy No. 4 is the focal point of long-range planning in many companies, and such firms seem to concentrate their planning on mergers and/or acquisitions, giving somewhat less emphasis to market development and product development, and no attention at all (in long-range planning) to operations improvement. Motorola's Director of Long-Range Planning (now Vice President, Planning) stated that Strategy No. 4 was more glamorous than the others, especially insofar as it pointed to mergers and acquisitions, but it was also more risky and was therefore not primarily emphasized in his company. He added that if Strategies No. 2 and No. 3 are followed, "you're moving with one foot on the ground and the chances of success are greater than with Strategy No. 4."

Motorola apparently believed that in balancing between all these strategies, the most important emphasis in organized long-range planning should be on Strategy No. 1, with somewhat less emphasis on Strategies No. 2 and No. 3. However, Motorola did not neglect "new product" research and development which can and often will lead to diversification opportunities. Motorola's additional diversification in the near term future will probably be concentrated on internal development as an outgrowth of Strategies No. 2 and/or No. 3, and not on mergers and/or acquisitions.

	EXISTING PRODUCTS	NEW PRODUCTS
EXISTING MARKETS	Strategy No. 1 - Operations Improvement	Strategy No. 3 - Product Development
NEW MARKETS	Strategy No. 2 - Market Development	Strategy No. 4 - Diversification

Figure 3: Strategies Available to Business Firms in a Product-Market Matrix

When formalized long-range planning was introduced in the company, President Galvin, the Chief Executive Officer, presented the concept orally to about 150 of the company's top managers. He defined formal planning, explained why it was essential for management, and stated that it was an inseparable part of every operating manager's job. He concluded his remarks by discussing a critical question—"How formal should long-range planning be?" His answer, reproduced in part as follows, provides a useful insight into the philosophy of planning in Motorola:

> Real artfulness is needed in determining how good, how realistic, and how complete plans must be. If allowed to be too loose, especially at the start, those who will be expected to accomplish the plans will quickly know planning has been inadequate, and they will therefore conclude that management's statements concerning planning were really not sincere. On the other hand, long-range planning cannot be done successfully by edict alone. It must have the full support of operating management at all levels. It must be simple enough and yet complete enough so that participation will not hinder the manager from doing his regular job, but will actually help him do a better job.

This statement, which calls for discipline, balance, and flexibility in long-range planning, reflects the broader concept of decentralized management which was practiced in Motorola. This philosophy has considerable merit, and its successful application hinges to a large degree on the capabilities and attitudes of the key managers who are involved. Mr. Galvin recognized this critical factor in one of his closing remarks when he stated that "the procedures and methods must fit the personalities of both the company and of the principal people who will be involved." Thus, features of the planning systems of other companies were "adapted" in Motorola, but not "adopted."

STEPS IN PLANNING

The day after the oral introduction of formalized planning in Motorola in 1962, each of the key managers was provided with a written copy of the President's remarks. An explanation of the basic elements of the conceived planning system was attached, as well as instructions for preparing formal plans and an annual schedule of planning activities. The planning steps and corresponding time schedules which have been utilized in the company in subsequent years are summarized in Table 5, and each step is explained in the following paragraphs.

TABLE 5

PLANNING STEPS AND SCHEDULE IN MOTOROLA INC.

Step	*Planning Activity*	*Time Schedule*
I	Set corporate profit growth goals	By January 1
II	Prepare "Prime Assumptions" about the environment	By January 1
III	Prepare "Divisional Assumptions"	By April 1
IV	Prepare tentative divisional five-year forecasts	By April 1
V	Review and challenge the tentative forecast of each division	April, May
VI	Revise and finalize divisional five-year forecasts	By June 1
VII	Prepare corporate five-year forecast	June
VIII	Determine extent of corporate "planning gap"	July
IX	Develop corporate plans to fill "planning gap"	July
X	Assign profit goals to each division	By August 1
XI	Determine extent of divisional "planning gaps"	August
XII	Develop and review divisional objectives and goals	By November 1

SETTING GOALS

Step I in the formalized planning process was the establishment of corporate growth goals by the Chief Executive Officer and the Board of Directors. These goals were initially expressed in terms of the desired growth in the earnings per share of common stock. Then they were specified in dollars of net profit and finally in dollars of profit-before-tax. This latter unit became the basic operating growth goal. Such profit goals were set for each of the next five years, and a profit target for the tenth year in the future was also specified.

These goals were set at what was considered an optimum level, where the risk of instability (or failure) from excessive growth was balanced against the risk of stagnancy from inadequate growth. The reason for setting numerical corporation goals as the initial step in planning was stated as follows: "A corporate profit growth goal, whatever it is, however arbitrarily set, will at least provide knowledge and a challenge." A reference standard for rate-of-return goals was derived from the actual performance figures for a "control group" of 15 selected corporations.

STATING ASSUMPTIONS

The next planning activity (Step II) was the preparation of a brief set of "Prime Assumptions" about the future external business environment. These assumptions were formulated by the Chief Executive Officer and the Director of Long-Range Planning. After review and approval by the Board of Directors, they were sent to the General Manager of each division and to other key executives to provide a uniform basis for long-range planning. These assumptions were apparently well in mind when corporate profit goals were set, for the expected future environment was a major determinant of the feasibility of such goals.

The "Prime Assumptions—January 1, 1965" were approved by the Board of Directors on December 1, 1964, and distributed immediately thereafter. They included a list of 14 assumptions on trends and expectations by 1970 in the areas of international tensions, international business, and domestic affairs. A table of assumed statistical data on population, income, and spending levels in the United States for each of the next six years and for the tenth year was attached. Corresponding actual figures for each of the past five years were also displayed. Estimates of the population, the number of households, and the civilian labor force in the United States for the year 2000 were also given.

In addition to these external factors which would affect the entire business, other external and internal variables were expected to affect various divisions in different ways. Thus, a set of "Divisional Assumptions" was prepared by each division to reflect such future expectations (Step III). These assumptions were formulated for each definable market and each product line. Information in newspapers and other current sources provided the basis for these "Divisional Assumptions." The "Prime Assumptions" were not considered too meaningful as inputs to divisional assumptions and plans, but provided general information. Projected Gross National Product values were not the basis for action in Motorola, and a bank economist, instead of staff specialists, provided advice on the economic outlook.

PREPARING AND REVIEWING FIVE-YEAR FORECASTS

On the basis of these two sets of assumptions, each division then prepared a tentative "five-year forecast" for sales, profits, and returns on investments in each of the next five years, as expected from a continuation of the existing business activities (Step IV). Corresponding actual data for the preceding five years and estimates for the current year were also given. The forecasts were not expected to reflect fluctuations in general economic activity in any given year, but instead, the growth trend over a five-year period was the element of greatest concern. In such forecasting, "normal" conditions were assumed for each year, where "normal" was the equivalent of "standard volume" in the automobile industry.

Review meetings were held in which a group of top executives challenged and discussed the tentative five-year forecast of each division separately (Step V). The review committee in 1965 included the Chairman of the Board of Directors, the President, the Vice President, Finance, and the Director of Long-Range Planning. When the forecast of a given division was reviewed and discussed, the General Manager of that division and two or three of his assistants attended and presented their data. They reviewed their five-year forecast in detail, as well as underlying assumptions and the relation of projections to past divisional results. Alternative courses of action, as well as corresponding expected results, were also presented and discussed.

The members of the review committee expressed their opinions on the relative merits of alternative proposals and on the accuracy of various projections by each division. After these challenge and review meetings, the divisional plans were sometimes revised to reflect the tenor of the comments by top executives. However, each General Manager was free to "stick" with his original forecast. In either case, the five-year forecasts for existing activities of each division were finalized (Step VI), and they were submitted to the corporate accounting staff for consolidation into a "Corporate Five-Year Forecast" (Step VII).

FINDING AND FILLING "PLANNING GAPS"

After the six divisional forecasts were combined, the projected growth of existing business activities for the entire corporation was compared to the corporate profit growth goal which was set in the first step of the planning sequence (Step VIII). If the projected growth did not equal the growth goal, a "planning gap" existed. The Director of Long-Range Planning in Motorola met with the Board of Directors at this point to look for a "planning gap" and to discuss its size and nature, if one existed. This step was considered "the start of real long-range planning," for all strategic objectives and plans were developed from this basic analysis.

To fill a corporate "planning gap," the company could attempt to diversify or it could "assign" additional growth to one or more existing divisions. After diversification opportunities were evaluated and any promising ones were selected to fill part of the "gap" (Step IX), each division of the company was assigned a profit goal for each of the next five years and also a ten-year profit target (Step X). These goals were in units of dollars of profit and percentage rate of return on investments.

At this point, goals were compared to divisional forecasts (Step XI), and any "planning gap" for each division (profit goals minus profit projections) became concrete. Divisional long-range planning then began in earnest, as ways to fill the "gaps" were sought.

Developing Specific Goals and Plans

The final step in the planning process in Motorola (Step XII) was to develop specific long-range plans to achieve divisional profit goals. The primary and essential technique for such divisional planning was to develop a framework of specific objectives and goals. Then operating and resource plans were built on and around these divisional expectations.

The format for summarizing and reviewing objectives and goals was adopted from an "Objectives and Goals Program" which had been in effect since 1958 in the company. The terminology and procedures of this program were familiar to managers, so it was improved and retained as part of the broader long-range planning system which was adopted in 1962. These more specific aspects of divisional planning are described in the following section.

DIVISIONAL PLANNING TERMINOLOGY, PROCEDURES, AND FORMATS

Planning Terminology

An "objective" was defined in Motorola as "a fundamental, endless, and continuing element of growth." It was considered to be "something really important that a division or department was striving to accomplish." The related term "goal" was defined as "a measurable portion of an objective, which must include a date and be accomplished by assignment of responsibility." Thus, a goal was a specific quantitative element of a broader continuing objective.

The formulation of objectives and goals by each operating unit in the company was focused on nine "Key Areas" of management responsibility. These areas are listed and defined, with most of the definitions quoted directly from company documents:

1. *Organization*—the way the major functional and/or product elements of the business relate to one another and to major tasks of the business,
2. *Management*—the adequacy (related to long-range goals) of the people in the first two or three levels—those who make the major decisions and supply key leadership,

3. *People*—the adequacy (related to long-range goals) of the people who perform the essential operational and supporting functions in the business,
4. *Technology*—the level of engineering and scientific skills and the accumulated amount of pertinent technical know-how possessed by the Engineering Department,
5. *Products*—that which is offered to the customers,
6. *Distribution*—the system for making products available to customers in adequate quantities whenever and wherever they are desired,
7. *Operations*—the efficiency and effectiveness with which the day-to-day activities of the business are conducted and controlled; this includes, but is not limited to: cost control, paperwork flow, productivity, etc.,
8. *Facilities*—the equipment, buildings, and auxiliary items which are necessary to develop and manufacture the company's products and to operate the business,
9. *Policies*—the significant attitudes which the business characteristically takes toward its customers, employees, and products; this includes, but would not be limited to: quality of products, warranty, extension of credit, etc.

DIVISIONAL PLANNING PROCEDURES AND FORMAT

When the time arrived in Motorola for the final step in planning—developing divisional objectives and goals—each General Manager wrote down the major strengths and weaknesses of his operating unit with respect to each of the nine "Key Areas." He then wrote *one* objective which pertained to each strength or weakness he had listed, with his focus on how to meet his profit goals by utilizing divisional strengths or by correcting divisional weaknesses. Any one General Manager might decide that he needed to concentrate his objectives in only two, three, or four of the "Key Areas." Therefore, he would give more attention to those areas where the need and potential for improvement were greatest.

After major objectives were listed, one or more goals were established to support each objective. Such goals provided tangible targets and reference standards for measuring the progress toward the realization of each broader objective. A target date for attainment and the responsible individual were specified for each goal.

These data were summarized on a special form to insure uniformity and to facilitate periodic reviews of progress. This format was the one which was adopted from the previous "Objectives and Goals Program." Excerpts from a hypothetical set of objectives and goals which were

Table 6: Illustration of Division Objectives, Goals, and Planning Format in Motorola, Inc.

BUSINESS MACHINES DIVISION (HYPOTHETICAL)

OBJECTIVES AND GOALS SEPTEMBER 1,1966 (DATE)

OBJECTIVES	GOALS	TARGET DATE	PRIME RE-SPONSIBILITY[b]	STATUS ON ____(DATE)
PROFIT-RETURN ON INVESTMENT[a] 1. Maximize short-term and long-term profits and return on investment to the extent possible in view of corporate policy and other objectives.	1.1 Profits of: $2,850,000 (8.7% on $33,000,000) $3,120,000 (9% on $34,700,000) $3,650,000 (10% on $36,500,000) $4,210,000 (11% on $38,300,000) $4,850,000 (12% on $40,300,000)	1967 1968 1969 1970 1971	Division Manager	
DISTRIBUTION[a] 2. Maintain and improve the effectiveness of and market penetration gained through existing sales branches.	2.1 Establish a five-year series of goals covering sales volume, market penetration, and expense ratios for each company branch.	6-30-67	Sales Manager and Branch Managers	
	2.2 Construct detailed written plans to accomplish goals in 2.1. Show: Markets to be served Additional investment required Merchandising programs Manpower needed - at all levels Training and/or recruitment plans.	12-31-67	Branch Managers	
PRODUCTS 3. Maintain Motorola's position of offering the best values (features, reliability, price and styling) in printing calculators and full keyboard adding machines in the industry.	3.1 Introduce basic new printing calculator models.	9-01-67 9-01-70	Chief Engineer, Product Manager, and Sales Manager	
	3.2 Introduce basic new full keyboard adding machines.	12-30-66 9-01-69		
	3.3 For the new models, establish master plans showing where and how we intend to carry over common tooling, assemblies, and piece parts. This program is expected to reduce the per unit tooling and start-up cost by at least 25% in 1968 as compared with 1965.	5-30-67	Product Planning Manager and Chief Engineer	
OPERATIONS[a] 4. Through intensified mechanization and facility study programs, maintain -- and, if possible, improve -- our position of having the lowest cost manufacturing operations in our industry.	4.1 Prepare a five year manufacturing plan, covering 1967 through 1971, showing additional mechanization, new machinery, recommended equipment design approaches (for cost savings) together with anticipated investment and cost savings.	4-30-67	Production Manager	

[a] "Key Area" Category

[b] Actual names are used in practice instead of titles

distributed to each divisional General Manager in Motorola to aid him in planning are shown in Table 6. The format of this table reflects the design of the actual forms utilized in the company for long-range planning.

Each General Manager submitted his proposed objectives and goals for the next five years to the top executives about September 1, along with his list of divisional strengths and weaknesses. A review meeting was scheduled for each division which was attended in 1965 by the Chairman of the Board of Directors, the President, the Director of Long-Range Planning, and the division's General Manager. This group spent a full day in discussing the proposed objectives, goals, and related plans. In addition, they reviewed the division's performance in the current year and the progress on previous goal attainment.

The Chief Executive Officer sometimes requested revisions in the proposals from each division, and he approved all objectives and goals before they were issued in final form. The six sets of approved objectives and goals from as many divisions constituted the "Long-Range Plan" in Motorola.

The planning procedures within each division in the company varied somewhat, since each General Manager decided how to plan. One division required a statement of objectives and goals from each department within the division on the same type of form which was used for divisional proposals (See Table 6). Another division used a different, more detailed form for departmental planning, while a third required no written objectives and goals from its sub-units.

THE RELATION OF BUDGETS TO LONG-RANGE PLANS

As soon as long-range objectives and goals were approved, each division prepared an operating budget, a cash budget, and a capital equipment budget for the coming year. To insure that the proposed budgets for 1965 were related closely to previous projections, the Budget Department sent forms to each operating unit in October, 1964, with the first two of three columns filled out. In the first column, the estimated actual figures (expenses, sales, revenues, etc.) for 1964 were given. In the next column, the corresponding figures for 1965, which were submitted during March, 1964, in the divisional "five-year forecasts" were also given. The third column was left blank for entry of the proposed budget figures for 1965 by the operating managers.

Thus, any deviations in the proposed budget from previous forecasts were obvious, and might have to be justified in the subsequent budget review meetings. In this manner, short-range financial planning and long-range planning were closely related. Budgets were submitted at the end of the planning cycle (about November 1) and were reviewed, revised, and approved by the end of December for the following year.

LONG-RANGE MANPOWER PLANNING FORMAT

A new form entitled "Management Staffing and Replacement" was used for the first time in 1964, and it "highlighted" the important area of management development in long-range corporate planning. Mr. Hickey said that "it focused more attention on more important areas than anything else that had been done."

This form was used in each division and in each department to summarize the status of key managers and potential replacements for them. It provided space for listing the job titles of 12 key positions in a vertical column. Horizontally and to the right, spaces were provided for the name of the incumbent in each position, his age, salary, and qualification in the present job (two ratings—present and potential—measured in units from 0 to 100 per cent). On the same horizontal lines, the name of the most qualified available replacement was listed for each position, as well as his name, salary, present job title, and promotability to the specified job (two ratings—present and potential—measured in units from 0 to 100 per cent).

The use of this form indicated clearly the needs for management personnel in future periods of time. If it was used regularly, such needs were recognized before they became critical and the required development or recruitment action could be initiated.

EVALUATION OF THE LONG-RANGE PLANNING SYSTEM

When formal long-range planning was introduced in Motorola in 1962, some officers and directors adopted a "wait and see" attitude. Some managers had their "guard up," for they thought it would interfere with doing their job relative to current operations. Others were "figure-oriented," and skeptical of an approach which focused on specific objectives and goals in various "Key Areas" of management. Therefore, formal planning was approached "gingerly."

BENEFITS OF FORMAL LONG-RANGE PLANNING

The Director of Long-Range Planning, who made the observations previously mentioned, stated that "there is 100 per cent acceptance today (more than two years after introduction) by the people involved in long-range planning." He added that "they realize it helps them do a better job and this is the only purpose of it."

When the decision was made to formalize long-range planning, Mr. Hickey spent a year studying the planning systems in various companies. He found strong and weak elements in different approaches, and tried to incorporate the very best ones in the system which was developed, accepted, and introduced by top management in Motorola. After a three-year test of the system, it seemed to be working well, and the company executives believed it was very beneficial.

Several distinct features were evident in the long-range planning system in Motorola, and many of them were unique among the 45 companies studied. Several of these features which should lead to beneficial results are summarized in the following paragraphs.

First, the basic premise which provided the foundation for the system was that "long-range planning is a discipline like organizing, motivating, controlling, etc." and is therefore a primary function of operating (line) managers. The key planning coordinator in Motorola felt that many staff planners believe it is their job to do long-range planning, and since they are increasing in number in many corporations in the United States, their biased point of view dominates many recent studies, meetings, and publications. He also believed that most long-range plans were weakened considerably because they were not prepared by line managers. He criticized staff planners in general for seeking to build up the importance of their job by issuing reports and building large staffs. The fact that this planning director had no assistants "punctuated" the belief by Motorola that line managers were responsible for long-range planning.

Another important feature of Motorola's planning system was the dominant role of profit goals—for the corporation and for each operating unit—as the beginning point in long-range planning. Profit goals could be called the "spear tip" of the planning thrust in the company. All subsequent objectives, sub-goals, and operational plans were made with the focus on achieving the initial profit goals.

In Motorola's planning process, the future status and profit potential of current operations were appraised carefully before efforts were made to diversify. Performance improvements were sought by utilizing valuable current resources and by overcoming current limitations instead of seeking new ventures at the beginning of the planning cycle. If a "gap" was found to exist between goals for the future and expected future profits from existing operations, then efforts were made to close the "gap" in the best possible way—new ventures, product development, or market development. The benefit of this approach was that profits were increased by giving proper attention to existing activities in long-range plans, instead of spending an undue amount of effort on more exciting, but more risky, new activities or acquisitions.

The requirement for written objectives and related goals was a vital element in Motorola's planning procedure. This technique forced managers to evaluate current performance and alternative future actions very carefully, and thereby led to more efficient performance. Since many goals were set by the managers who sought to achieve them, a self-imposed inducement and an obligation to perform well were also created.

The subdivision of the total spectrum of management functions and responsibilities into nine "Key Areas" to serve as bases for setting objectives and planning activities was also very beneficial. This procedure insured that one or another important aspect of long-range planning would not be neglected.

The systematic nature of the planning system in Motorola also deserved much credit. The major steps in planning were clearly specified, as were the responsibility assignments and the planning time schedule. In this system, all those involved knew what was expected and when, and the discipline of formality prevented unnecessary delays or procrastination. The written definitions of key planning terms also insured more uniform interpretations and more consistent presentations. Planning completely "how to plan," or developing the planning system, was done carefully, and this step undoubtedly led to more efficient performance.

The format used for summarizing objectives and goals (Table 6) was a valuable element in Motorola's system. It was simple, but carefully designed to obtain more effective planning and control. In addition to the space for written objectives and goals, it required the name of the person who was responsible and the target date for achievement of each goal. A blank space was provided for reporting periodically the progress toward goal realization, so that a built-in mechanism existed for review and control.

Performance control was an integral part of the planning system. Progress on preceding goals was reviewed annually by top executives when future goals were being set. In addition, divisional personnel were requested to review the progress on their objectives and goals at monthly operations review meetings. The Board of Directors was active in planning and reviewing performance, for it was relatively small and was composed largely of company executives. Thus, control from the top was ever-present in Motorola's planning system, and in many respects, it was similar to a system which has been called "Integrated Planning and Control."[1]

Another factor which contributed to more effective long-range planning in Motorola was the long experience of the Director of this function in the organization. He had worked 15 years for the company and knew the products and people well. He believed that knowing the business and the people and how they related to one another was essential for effective coordination of planning efforts. Conversely, he felt it was a mistake to obtain such a staff specialist from outside of the company, and suggested such action as a likely reason for the fact that some companies which formalized planning in recent years were not entirely satisfied with their results.

POTENTIAL LIMITATIONS OF FORMAL LONG-RANGE PLANNING

Some potential limitations existed in the decentralized planning system in Motorola. The lack of staff specialists for economic analysis, operations research, and other planning functions might result in serious oversights or inadequate attention to important aspects of long-range planning. However, one division in the company had established a function entitled Director of Planning, and more staff specialists may be utilized as a need for them becomes evident.

Another limitation in a system such as Motorola's results from the degree of decentralized authority. When the manager of each operating unit has wide latitude in choosing the extent, degree, and methodology of his planning efforts, wide variations in planning effectiveness may exist between various units. Such a system permits individual managers to innovate and to develop procedures and plans which might be stifled by a rigid imposed system, but it also permits less competent or aggressive managers to be less effective than desired and gives them "enough rope to hang themselves." The net value of such results is uncertain in any situation, but the company could be harmed seriously if control procedures were not quick and sure.

GENERAL APPRAISAL OF MOTOROLA'S LONG-RANGE PLANNING SYSTEM

The ideal organization structure for long-range planning, as well as for other functions of business management, should maximize the efficiency and effectiveness of the firm in attaining its objectives through an optimum combination of line and staff assignments. The benefits of each should be maximized and the disadvantages should be minimized. This view is implicit in currently-accepted management theory, but a company is never certain in practice when it attains this optimum point. Motorola relied primarily on operating managers for long-range planning, but overall, their system had many outstanding features. Therefore, it seems highly probable that many business firms in the United States could benefit greatly by adopting such a simple, straight-forward system.

Footnotes for Chapter 5

[1] For a detailed description of this system, see John O. Tomb, "A New Way to Manage—Integrated Planning and Control," *California Management Review,* V, No. 1 (Fall, 1962), 57–62.

Chapter 6

Long-Range Planning in a Major Automobile Company

The long-range planning system in a firm which is one of the major producers of motor vehicles in the United States and in the world is described in this chapter. This firm is also an important producer of defense, space, and other diversified products, but it is identified herein only by the pseudoname "Carco."

NATURE OF MOTOR VEHICLE MANUFACTURING

The current operating pattern in the automotive industry is for general product specifications to be formulated approximately four years before the finished vehicle is ready for sale. Model changes occur every year due to the competitive struggle between producers to offer a product with greater styling appeal and better technical performance. Thus, various continuing activities take place simultaneously in each auto company which are related to producing and marketing vehicles in the coming year, as well as two, three, and four years in the future. In addition, some of the current research efforts are expected to culminate in engineering improvements on models which are five, six, or seven years away.

Thus, an extensive amount of planning is necessary to provide the styling, research, engineering, tooling, production facilities, marketing systems, financial resources, and skilled personnel to produce motor vehicles of proper quality, quantity, and price to satisfy an uncertain level and type of demand at future points in time and space. To make the job more difficult, all of this is required while facing intense competition, a changing business environment, and the need to realize satisfactory profits.

This four-year planning cycle for new vehicle development and production is probably one of the longest in any consumer-product industry. It is properly called long-range planning, but it pertains in large part to a series of one-cycle operational and capital investment plans. Motor vehicles constitute the major product lines, and the basic demand pattern for this type of product does not change rapidly, as for some other consumer goods. Thus, the focal point of long-range planning is on existing operations instead of changes in basic strategy. However, marketing strategy, product styling, engineering, and basic design are important planning variables. Also, diversification and development of other product lines are important, but not dominant, aspects of planning.

Facilities planning is a very important aspect of long-range planning in the auto industry, for as demand increases and technology advances, each producer has to provide adequate production capacity and also remain competitive on the basis of cost per unit. Production plants have to be designed and started many months before the date they are needed, just as equipment and tooling have to be ordered far in advance. Plant requirements in a given company are determined by forecasting the total future demand and then deciding what fraction of the total market sales the company will try to obtain. Production capacity is then sought to provide the "target" output rate during a selected future period of time. However, some flexibility is possible by more (or less) intensive utilization of existing facilities.

ORGANIZATION FOR LONG-RANGE PLANNING

LONG-RANGE PLAN COMMITTEE

Long-range planning was formalized in Carco in 1963. Primary responsibility was assigned to a Long-Range Plan Committee which was composed of four staff Vice Presidents. This committee was accountable to the President, and its stated objective was to "develop corporate long-range plans and objectives, revise as necessary, and monitor adherence." The Vice President —Finance—was the chairman of this committee, and it met at his request.

The Long-Range Plan Committee was essentially a reviewing, approving, and recommending body. Specific duties, as stated in the organization manual at Carco, were:

1. Strengthen and refine long-range planning techniques and extend planning concepts to include all phases of long-range operational and financial planning;
2. Working with the operating groups and the corporate staffs, reconcile long-range operational requirements with anticipated cash levels and long-range revenue, cost, and profit factors, and develop a comprehensive "Long-Range Plan";
3. Make adjustments to segments of the "Plan" as required and resolve disagreements or problems which may arise during the development of the "Plan";
4. Present the "Long-Range Plan" to the President and the Administrative Committee for review and approval; [1]
5. Revise and update the "Long-Range Plan" as necessary;
6. Review and approve the allocation of corporate funds on a time-phased priority basis according to the needs of the corporation; and
7. Review progress of the corporation and its components in carrying out the approved "Long-Range Plan," take corrective action as required, and keep the President and concerned Administrative Committee members advised.

CORPORATE FINANCIAL STAFF ASSIGNMENTS

The key long-range planning coordinator in Carco was the Manager of the Investment Analysis Department in the Corporate Comptroller's Office, and he provided most of the factual data which are included in this chapter. He worked closely with the Long-Range Plan Committee, and technically he reported to its chairman through the Comptroller. This close structural link was beneficial for effective coordination of planning activities, especially since the Comptroller did not expect all discussions and correspondence between the Manager of Investment Analysis and the Vice President-Finance to be channeled through him.

The Investment Analysis Department had important analytical and coordinating assignments in Carco's long-range planning system. The basic purpose of this corporate staff group was "to help management in allocating limited funds to those facility, tooling, and other nonrecurring expenditures that best assure the achievement of planned short- and long-range operating goals." To fulfill this purpose, the 16-member department was formally responsible for the coordination, development, and administration of:

1. long-range operating plans (joint effort with Corporate Profit Analysis Department),
2. short-range and long-range capital plans,
3. a system for review and approval of project appropriation, lease and disposal requests,
4. management information and control reports, and
5. post-completion evaluation of project appropriations.

The importance of capital investments in long-range planning in the automobile industry was a primary reason for the assignment of formal planning responsibility to the Investment Analysis Department. However, the activities of this group were not restricted to long-range planning, as indicated in the preceding list of duties. Approximately two man-years of the group's total effort were spent on this function annually.

The Profit Analysis Department, also in the Comptroller's Office, had an important role in long-range planning. The function of this group, as indicated by their name, was to analyze projected profits in proposed long-range plans and to suggest ways to improve profits in unacceptable plans. They also consolidated the financial projections in long-range plans which were prepared by each operating unit in the corporation. Then, they summarized these data for analysis by the Long-Range Plan Committee and the Administrative Committee.

Financial planning and control were the primary focal points in all long-range planning activities in Carco. This fact accounted for the important role of the Comptroller's staff, who were directly involved in planning in each operating unit and at the corporate level.

OTHER CORPORATE STAFF ASSIGNMENTS

The Corporate Manufacturing Engineering Office also fulfilled a key role in long-range planning in Carco. The Director of this unit reported to the Vice President-Operations Staff, who was one of the members of the Long-Range Plan Committee. The function of this group was indicated by its name, and various members served as "Review Coordinators" to help different operating and staff units in the company develop long-range plans. They spent as much as five or ten per cent of their time on long-range planning, and this effort was primarily for facility planning. Manufacturing Engineering staffs were also located in various organizational sub-units, and they filled the same role at the lower levels as the corporate staff did for major units such as groups, divisions, or subsidiaries.

The Corporate Manufacturing Engineering staff was financially oriented, and they worked closely with the Investment Analysis Department in evaluating capital investment proposals. In fact, these two groups submitted jointly-determined recommendations to the Long-Range Plan Committee on proposed plans, even though the latter group made the physical presentation.

Other corporate staff groups also performed important long-range planning functions. The Business Research Office made short- and long-range economic forecasts of the future business environment. Then the Market Planning Office forecast industry and company sales for future periods of time by market segments and product lines, using a complex mathematical model.

The Product Planning Offices [2] developed basic specifications for future vehicles, and they also published product and volume assumptions, using data from the Market Planning Office. These assumptions provided a foundation for long-range planning by the operating units.

RESPONSIBILITIES OF OPERATING MANAGERS AND EXECUTIVES

In spite of the dominant role of corporate staff groups, long-range planning in Carco was considered an integral part of every operating manager's job and not the exclusive function of one department or person. An extensive amount of staff assistance and coordination was necessary because of the integrated nature of motor vehicle manufacturing and due to the basic functional organization structure in Carco. The central staffs determined the vehicles and volumes to be produced, and line managers utilized their own valuable operating experience in developing long-range plans to do the job efficiently. They also approved specific plans at successive levels in the organization's hierarchy, with top executives making the final decisions.

The President of Carco was enthusiastic about long-range planning and provided dynamic leadership in making it effective. He set "profit improvement" goals and reviewed planning activities informally as they progressed. He was called "the key reviewer and activator of control procedures to improve," and also played a dominant role in the approval or disapproval of recommended long-range plans. The President and Chairman of the Board of Directors worked together closely, and they assumed personal responsibility for investigating potential acquisitions or profitable extensions of company activities.

The organization for long-range planning in Carco included almost everyone in a managerial or staff position, even though the groups discussed above were most actively engaged in this effort. Several top-level functional committees were also involved in planning. This extensive involvement resulted from the emphasis on operational and facility planning, which in turn reflected the nature of the industry and the dominant role of one product line in the company.

PURPOSE AND EVOLUTION OF LONG-RANGE PLANNING

The stated intent of long-range planning in Carco was to develop an operational plan which:

1. helps to anticipate problems before they occur,
2. specifies significant operating objectives,
3. details the steps and actions necessary to meet objectives,
4. projects the financial consequences of forward operating plans,
5. establishes a reference point against which specific operating proposals can be measured, and
6. provides a continuing improvement in corporate profits.

The tangible result of such planning was called the "Long-Range Plan," and it was defined as "a consolidation of operational and financial plans compiled from all areas of the corporation."

When long-range planning was formalized in Carco, the first cycle of planning activity (1963-1964) produced a "Long-Range Plan" which included capital investment proposals for four years and the projected financial results from planned operations during the next three years. Subsequently, the total capital requirements for the corporation, as specified in the "Long-Range Plan," were considered excessive for various reasons, and several investment proposals were postponed or rejected. This action required an extensive revision of the operational plans and corresponding financial projections.

In order to make planning efforts more efficient, a new two-phase planning procedure was developed and introduced in the 1964-1965 planning cycle. This procedure called for the submission of capital investment proposals only in Phase I. These proposals were based on preliminary product and volume assumptions for future years. They pertained only to the buildings, equipment, tooling, etc. needed for expansion, new models, and new products, or to funds required for acquisitions or investments in securities. However, over 90 per cent of the total corporate capital expenditures were made in these categories.

After the preliminary determinations of total capital spending were made and approved, a "Capital Plan" was issued. This step was completed before detailed operational planning was started. In Phase II, a complete "Long-Range Plan" was developed which included an operational plan, a profit plan, and a final capital plan. This sequence of planning activities eliminated the unnecessary effort expended in revising plans.

The Chairman of the Long-Range Plan Committee stated the advantage of this system in a memorandum to operating managers when the new procedure was introduced. He said:

This two-step approach to long-range planning should provide an early opportunity to evaluate the effect on capital expenditures of preliminary product plans, tooling volumes, sourcing plans and operating patterns. Revisions deemed necessary at this stage of development will not entail the subsequent effort necessary to revise complete, detailed Long-Range Plans.

PHASE I PLANNING—CAPITAL PLANS

PLANNING ASSUMPTIONS AND INSTRUCTIONS

The memorandum which introduced the two-phase planning procedure was sent to the group executive, division manager, or president of each operating unit in October, 1964. A 75-page manual entitled "Long Range Plan—Phase I Assumptions and Instructions" was distributed with the memo. The instructions pertained to the mechanics of preparing and submitting capital expenditure proposals for the next four model years (1966-1969), and to the requirements for data on manufacturing capacity and expansion potential. A model year extended from August 1 in one year through July 31 of the specified year.

Assumptions were provided about the use of facilities, tooling volumes, and operating patterns in making plans for future production needs. Assumptions about facilities pertained to the size, location, and timing of new or expanded facilities, and the relocation or deactivation of existing operations. Assumptions about "sourcing" (making or buying) components were also included in the Phase I planning manual. Sample formats for proposals were provided, and a timetable was given which listed each planning activity and specified the due date and the party responsible for completion of each step.

On the same day that planning instructions were issued, preliminary product plans, sales trend volumes, and tooling volumes were distributed by the Product Planning Office and the Product Analysis Department. The distribution of these basic assumptions was more restricted than for the planning instructions, and it was made on a "need to know" basis.

The instruction manual was prepared by the Investment Analysis Department, but the assumptions it included on "sourcing" plans and operating patterns were provided by the Corporate Manufacturing Engineering Office.

Copies of the planning instructions were sent to group or division comptrollers, as well as to first-level operating executives. Additional distributions were made to lower levels from the headquarters of each major organizational unit. The comptrollers in these units or their assistants served as coordinators for preparing capital plans, and each one received a supply of all necessary forms from the Investment Analysis Department. The forms were then distributed to sub-units in the organization by the coordinator in each major unit of the company.

PHASE I PLANNING PROCEDURES

Specific capital proposals and other required data were assembled by the comptroller in each operating unit after plans were formulated by engineering staffs and operating managers. When the responsible manager approved the "Capital Plan" for his unit, it was submitted to the next level in the organization for review, approval, and for combining with plans from other units. Finally, each group or division prepared a consolidated summary of their respective "Capital Plans," and the chief operating executive signed it to indicate his approval. Then all of the required data on capital investment proposals were submitted to the Investment Analysis Department for subsequent review. This step in the planning cycle occurred about five weeks after Phase I planning instructions were distributed.

During the last half of this interval, each of the 11 members of the Corporate Manufacturing Engineering Office who were designated as "Long-Range Plan Review Coordinators" worked with personnel in one or more assigned operating or staff units as they developed capital proposals. Each of these coordinators visited his assigned area as much as possible to review and discuss proposals, and two "coordinator progress report" meetings were held. After the capital plans from each unit were submitted to the Investment Analysis Department, they were sent to the Corporate Manufacturing Engineering Office for review and analysis by the "Review Coordinators."

Each "Long-Range Plan Review Coordinator" was responsible "for coordinating the review efforts of all Manufacturing Engineering Departments directed toward the assigned Group or Division Long-Range Plan." Each one conducted a formal review of the capital investment proposals which originated in his assigned area after he received them. These reviews were made in consultation with operating personnel, and were completed about one week after the capital proposals were submitted.

Then each "Review Coordinator" prepared a written "Review Report" and presented it orally to staff personnel at the highest level in his assigned area. He reported any proposed expenditures which were considered questionable or non-mandatory. Such debatable proposals were often pointed out initially in reviews by the Manufacturing Engineering staffs at lower levels in the organization. Each of the four departments [3] in the Corporate Manufacturing Engineering Office also reviewed the proposed capital plans and reported any questionable items to the proper Review Coordinator. After these staff review meetings were held for each major organizational unit, final recommendations of the Manufacturing Engineering Office and the Product Analysis Department were formulated.

A coordinator from the Investment Analysis Department was also assigned to participate in each Long-Range Plan Review, and each of these financial coordinators worked with the engineering coordinator for a designated organizational unit. The representatives of these two corporate staff groups reviewed the proposed capital plans in order to detect:

1. programs that did not conform to published sourcing, facility, or volume assumptions,
2. programs of different units which conflicted,
3. expenditures which seemed to be of unreasonable magnitude or improperly timed,
4. programs which did not contain adequate consideration of alternatives,
5. proposals which were incomplete or which contained inadequate data,
6. unsatisfactory explanations of major changes in estimates from those of the prior year, and
7. less than optimum use of facilities and capital funds, in view of the corporation financial objectives and sound planning principles.

Recommendations for revisions in the proposed capital plans were agreed upon by the Manufacturing Engineering Office and the Investment Analysis Department at corporate headquarters. These recommendations were finalized a few weeks after the original capital plans were submitted. Then the Investment Analysis and Profit Analysis Departments developed projections of the sources and applications of funds, based on known and estimated data. These projections were submitted with the proposed capital plans and the recommended capital plan revisions to the Long-Range Plan Committee. This group reviewed the plans and approved some or all of the recommendations.

Their recommendations were then submitted to the President for his consideration. After reviewing the level of total proposed capital expenditures and the available sources of funds, the President, the Administrative Committee, and the Board of Directors approved the "Capital Plan" for the corporation. If changes in specific plans were required during the review by top executives, the key staff and operating managers met and worked out the details together.

The capital spending proposals for the 1966 model year were considered most carefully, and priorities were designated for the projected capital expenditures of each operating unit. For the corporation as a whole, about 40 per cent were classified as (previously) "approved programs or projects," 40 per cent were "necessary," 15 per cent were "economically desirable," and 5 per cent were "desirable." These priorities provided some flexibility in the amount of total approved capital spending.

The operating executives in each major unit were informed of the final approved "Capital Plan," and they notified the various managers in their respective units. These executives were informed previously of staff recommendations and many of them served on the Administrative Committee, so they were aware of developments and often directly involved. Phase I of the long-range planning procedure was completed early in 1965 when the "Capital Plan" for model years 1966 through 1969 was approved. However, this plan was a preliminary one, and the final capital spending proposals were included in the "Long Range Plan" which was developed in Phase II of the planning process.

PHASE II PLANNING—COMPLETE LONG-RANGE PLANS

Planning Assumptions and Instructions

In December, 1964, as soon as Phase I capital spending proposals were submitted for review, a manual entitled "1966 Long-Range Plan Instructions and Assumptions (Phase II)" was issued to each major operating unit in Carco by the Comptroller's Office. Several corporate staff groups cooperated in the preparation of this 3/4-inch-thick planning guide. It provided a common basis for preparing complete, detailed long-range plans in each group, division, and corporate staff office in the company. These specific instructions were expected to produce plans which were more uniform and more consistent internally. The requested plans were to cover all activities in the next three model years (1966, 1967, and 1968), a period which extended from August 1965 through July 1968.

Final product plans for all groups and divisions were published by the Product Planning Office by the end of 1964. About two weeks later, the recommendations of the Long-Range Plan Committee on capital expenditure levels for the next four years were published. These recommendations pertained to the proposals which were submitted in Phase I of the planning cycle. At this time, final product volumes, assumptions, and instructions were also issued. These documents and the initial manual of "Phase II Instructions and Assumptions" provided the essential framework for preparing formal long-range plans in each operating unit.

Long-range plans were also requested from each corporate staff office, and these staff plans were expected to correspond to the operational plans in time span. A memorandum containing additional planning instructions was sent to the director of each corporate staff function in January 1965, by the Managers of the Investment Analysis and Profit Analysis Departments jointly. The long-range plan from each of these staff units was requested in the form of an eight- to ten-page narrative which high-lighted:

1. significant operating objectives of the staff office,
2. steps and actions necessary to meet these objectives,
3. anticipated problems, and
4. financial consequences of forward operating plans.

A statistical summary of manpower, expense, and space requirements was to be included at the end of each narrative. Information on manpower and capital expenditure plans, data processing needs, and expense budgets was also requested from each staff unit in advance of their formal long-range plans. These data were needed by those staff units responsible for personnel, accounting, systems-procedures, and profit analysis, respectively.

Each group, division, and corporate office director was requested to appoint a "General Coordinator" for the preparation of long-range plans. The planning instruction manual and supplementary sections were distributed to the designated coordinator in each unit by the Investment Analysis Department, and distributions within the units were made by these "General Coordinators."

The assumptions provided for Phase II planning were similar to those used in Phase I, but were up-to-date and more detailed. They pertained primarily to products, volumes, operating patterns, facilities, and sourcing. Many of these assumptions were issued directly to the operating units by the staff group which prepared them and they were inserted or referenced in the instruction manual.

The instructions for preparing detailed long-range plans in Carco fell into two broad categories, pertaining either to functional plans or to financial plans. The instructions for various functional plans were prepared by the corporate staff which was responsible for each particular function. A planning coordinator from each of these groups was designated to review the functional plans which were prepared in various operating units before they were included in the final long-range plans.

NATURE OF FUNCTIONAL PLANS

Functional plans were prepared which pertained to finances, manufacturing and industrial engineering, marketing, organization, personnel, production programming, purchasing, quality and reliability, and other more specialized functions. These plans focused on specific objectives and methods to accomplish them. Time-phasing of various objectives was stressed, and specific problems, programs, and accomplishments were included in some functional plans.

The objectives in such plans often pertained to the internal operation of the functional unit—its organization, personnel training and utilization, or administrative procedures. In other cases, objectives referred to the performance efficiency or scope of broader functional activities within a given operating unit of the company. Manpower planning was also an important consideration in all of the functional plans.

NATURE OF FINANCIAL PLANS

The financial section of the long-range plans for each unit included a capital plan and a profit plan.

Capital Spending Plans

The capital expenditure schedules covered a period of five years—the current year and four forward years. A "Capital Plan Request Sheet" was prepared by each operating unit for every anticipated major project except those which were approved previously. Each request included a written description of the project, the expected level of each type of expenditure in each of five model years and all subsequent years, various accounting codes, and approval signatures.

Each operating unit was also required to submit standard schedules which projected various financial data, as: (1) changes in working capital, (2) analysis of changes in property, plant, and equipment, (3) write-down and sale of fixed assets, and (4) lease requests.

Capital plans were summarized by each unit on three forms. First, a general summary included the following numerical data for each of five model years:

1. total expenditures in each of three classes—facilities, special tools, and investments,
2. total expenditures for each of 12 reasons—new model, expansion, quality improvement, research and development, etc.,
3. total expenditures in each of four priority codes, and
4. changes in various types of working capital.

Approval signatures were required by the plant comptroller, plant manager, group comptroller, and group executive.

A second form included the expected capital expense for facilities and for special tools for each of six future models of passenger cars and trucks in each of six periods of time. The periods of time considered were: prior to August 1965; model year 1966; model year 1967; model year 1968; model year 1969; and after July 1969.

The third form summarized all of the capital projects which were proposed by the operating unit. Each individual project was summarized on a single line.

Each group and division in Carco also prepared consolidated summary schedules of the first two types described above, as well as a consolidated analysis of changes in property, plant, and equipment. Certain subsidiaries of the corporation prepared projected balance sheets, a schedule of sources and applications of funds, and a schedule of changes in cash and securities. Dollar amounts were given for each item in the schedules for the current model year and for each of the next four model years. Balance sheet data for the close of the preceding model year were also given.

A technical section was also included in the long-range capital plans. It contained data on existing manufacturing capacity and expected capacity requirements for major product lines and components for the current model year and for each of five future model years. In addition, information on the maximum expansion potential of each plant was provided on plot plans and narrative reports.

The final part of the technical section included "Expansion Proposal Data Sheets" which specified the reasons for expansion, the physical time-phasing of the program (as opposed to expenditure timing), and the type of expansion (extension, new location, purchase, lease, etc.). Alternative expansion methods, the effect of any volume adjustments on expansion plans, plot plans, etc. were given, and the forms were signed by the responsible manager of "manufacturing engineering."

These technical operational details provided the justification for proposed capital expenditures, and made long-range planning for future activities more meaningful and worthwhile. Without such data, "capital planning" could have been an exercise in arranging figures which had limited value.

Profit Plans

Profit plans were prepared by each organizational group or division as part of their long-range plans. Two sets of financial projections were made for each of the next three model years. One was based on a control volume and the other was based on a sales trend volume. Detailed instructions and sample formats were provided by the Profit Analysis Department of the Corporate Comptroller's Office in the manual of instructions for Phase II planning. Profit objectives were also specified by the Long-Range Plan Committee.

Seven standard financial schedules and supporting data were required from each major unit in Carco. These schedules included a financial summary which specified the number of product units, net sales ($), profits, per cent return on sales, and per cent return on assets—for the preceding year, current year, and three future years. Separate financial projections were included for "sales trend" plans and "control volume" plans. A profit variance summary, a manufacturing expense summary, and a sales detail schedule were also required. In addition, general and administrative expense schedules were required which included several cost change analyses, engineering expense, advertising and sales promotion media expense, an analysis of manpower changes, and a financial statement classification of projected expenditures. The comptroller and general manager of each unit signed the financial summary schedule in the long-range profit plan for their area of operations.

PROCEDURE FOR APPROVAL OF LONG-RANGE PLANS

The group and divisional staff heads reviewed operational narratives in long-range plans with their functional staff counterparts at the corporate level. Then the long-range plans from each group, division, and (staff) office were reviewed by the appropriate Vice Presidents and submitted to the Corporate Comptroller's Office. After review and consolidation, plans were sent to the Long-Range Plan Committee.

This group analyzed the plans carefully, and worked out refinements and revisions to improve projected profits. After several meetings, they approved the plans and presented them on slides to the Administrative Committee.

After the Administrative Committee reviewed and approved the plans, the action was recorded by the committee secretary. The principal operating executives served on this committee and received copies of the minutes which verified the approval of their long-range plans. Then each executive notified the key operational and staff personnel at lower levels in each respective unit. The 1964-1965 long-range planning cycle was completed in March, 1965.

NATURE OF THE "LONG-RANGE PLAN"

The "Long-Range Plan" for Carco was summarized in a booklet of 30 graphic schedules. The data in this document pertained to four major subjects:

1. Carco's volume objectives,
2. resources required to achieve the volume objectives,
3. financial results of the "Long-Range Plan" programs, and
4. benefits of attaining the planned programs.

THE RELATION OF BUDGETS AND LONG-RANGE PLANS

Budget forms for the next model year were distributed soon after the "Long-Range Plan" was finalized. The budgets were expected to include figures which corresponded to those in the "Long-Range Plan," but more detailed data were required.

EVALUATION OF THE LONG-RANGE PLANNING SYSTEM

BENEFITS OF FORMAL LONG-RANGE PLANNING

Formalized long-range planning in Carco, after two complete cycles, was considered to be very beneficial. Since the formal procedures were established, all correspondence and proposals pertaining to long-range planning were channeled through one office, the Investment Analysis Department. This action prevented the confusion and delays which had sometimes occurred previously when each of many different staff groups contacted various operating groups independently. Thus, coordination of activities was more effective and more efficient.

The President was very much "sold" on long-range planning and this was an important factor in making it effective. The procedure of submitting formal plans for future activities three or four years in advance enabled the President and other top executives to evaluate them more carefully and to seek improvements in projected results before firm commitments were made.

The formal plans also permitted more efficient allocation of capital funds. For example, expansions were scheduled so that the costs which would result from either excessive or insufficient manufacturing capacity were minimized. Existing facilities were also utilized more efficiently and the objective of profit improvement was given added emphasis by the development and review of formal plans. Managers at all levels were forced to think more systematically about the future impact of current decisions.

The two-phase planning cycle proved to be advantageous and will be continued. Since capital spending levels were proposed, adjusted, and approved in advance of detailed operational planning, a potential "tear-up" of specific plans was avoided. In some situations, this saving in time and effort could be significant. In the 1964-1965 planning cycle, the two-step procedure also was credited with speeding up the planning process so that the results were obtained 90 days earlier. By focusing on capital planning first, the subsequent operational planning was reported to be more carefully done. In addition, plans for obtaining any needed capital funds could be made sooner.

LIMITATIONS OF FORMAL LONG-RANGE PLANNING

Some limitations of Carco's long-range planning procedures were evident to those most directly involved. Communication was considered to be the major problem area, for many functional staff groups and operating managers at several levels in the corporation had planning responsibilities and needed to work together closely. Misunderstanding and inefficient communication resulted from the large number of persons involved in planning and from their widespread geographical dispersion. Many of these parties shared in the review of plans and in making decisions. Therefore, the extensive use of committees and the required agreement between various staff and operating groups seemed to create inherent inefficiencies in communication and action. The burden placed on "coordinators" was a heavy one.

The multiplicity of planning assignments in Carco resulted in large part from the nature of the company's activities and from its basic organization structure. The activities of the firm were highly integrated in the dominant area of motor vehicle production and marketing. A delicate balance was required between component production or purchase, final product assembly, and sales, so the decisions in one area had to be related carefully to those in other areas.

The activities in Carco were also organized to a large extent on a functional basis, and it was necessary to integrate much of the planning at corporate headquarters. The extensive utilization of staff personnel with functional responsibility and the centralized structure for planning and control made planning procedures more complex and coordination more difficult.

The experience in Carco during the early cycles of formalized planning revealed some limitations in the mechanics of the planning system which were to be corrected in future planning cycles. The planning schedule was expected to begin sooner, and more time was to be allocated for various groups to develop their long-range plans. More specific, detailed objectives were to be sought in future plans, and all responsible parties were to be encouraged to time-phase their objectives in relation to the expected dates for accomplishment. This procedure was to be applied to corporation-wide activities and to specific functional plans.

The tendency for some individuals to be vague and general about their plans for improvement was also evident to those who reviewed Carco's plans. In the future, more careful thinking on how and when to reach targets was to be sought. Improvements such as these are needed in any new planning system, and they should be realized gradually as new procedures evolve and old ones are refined.

Another problem which the Manager of the Investment Analysis Department reported was the difficulty of estimating future capital expenditures accurately. Decisions to "make or buy" may be reversed at times for various reasons, and capital needs often increase as products become more complex and diverse. In addition, production volumes change over time due to inaccurate forecasts of consumer tastes or purchasing power, and due to the actions of a competitor. No contingency for capital expenditures was provided in the first formal long-range plan in Carco, and when the need for additional capital outlays arose, some retiming of expenditures was necessary. Therefore, a contingency category was added to the second long-range capital plan.

The planning procedure in Carco was very complicated and the key planning coordinator felt that it should be simplified. The planning instructions were very detailed and the number of required forms was extensive. The Comptroller's Office developed most of the procedures which were required, and precise accounting conventions were prevalent. After the second planning cycle was completed, the corporate staff groups in the company were considering carefully the amount of detail and the degree of accuracy which was needed in future long-range projections.

In the third planning cycle, the same general concept and procedures for long-range planning were to be followed, but they were to be refined and simplified wherever staff and field effort could be reduced without a significant loss of benefit. The detailed financial projections for each year beyond the next one were likely to be discontinued. The criterion in Carco was to be—"Does the benefit justify the cost of the effort?"

GENERAL APPRAISAL

When long-range planning was formalized in the company, a new function was not established in the organizational structure. Instead, the required administrative and coordinating functions were assigned to existing staff groups with functional responsibilities. A valid question may be raised as to how to organize for the most effective long-range planning effort. Should it be in existing functional groups or in a separate planning function? No one can answer with certainty, and sound reasons can be given for either point of view.

A similar question pertains to the position of the key planning coordinator. Could a top-level planning officer serve more effectively than a Long-Range Plan Committee with functional staff assistants? The chief executive in any corporation should consider these questions, for the organization structure and planning procedures may be the most critical factors for successful forward planning.

Long-range planning in Carco was focused primarily on operational planning for one major product line which had an unsually long development period. Even though one type of product was dominant, the possible variations in this product were so vast that planning was very complex.

Facility planning in Carco was a major task with many alternatives available, and the capital spending levels for a given year were higher than most corporations attain in several years.

Product development efforts to improve performance or to advance technology were extensive, and market development was an important consideration. In addition, opportunities for merger, acquisition, diversification, or investment were carefully evaluated.

Thus, long-range planning in Carco was very broad in scope, in spite of the emphasis on existing operations. The formal planning procedure provided a method for improved management, and Carco was convinced that the benefits from the extra effort justified the costs.

Footnotes for Chapter 6

[1] The Administrative Committee was composed of top operating and staff executives. It met regularly and was active in short-range and long-range planning. It reviewed, approved, or disapproved major recommendations of the Long-Range Plan Committee.

[2] The Product Planning Offices (domestic and international) reported to the Vice President—Product Planning and Development—who was one of the members of the Long-Range Plan Committee.

[3] These departments were called: Source and Capacity Planning, Facilities Analysis and Planning, Industrial Engineering, and Production Engineering.

Chapter 7

Long-Range Corporate Planning in Transition

In this final chapter, the evolutionary pattern of change in long-range planning procedures within industrial corporations is reviewed, and some of the most significant current trends in formalized planning systems are summarized. Finally, an appraisal is made of the role of formalized long-range planning systems in business management.

EVOLUTION OF LONG-RANGE PLANNING SYSTEMS

The Pattern of Evolution Toward Formalized Planning

Long-range corporate planning procedures have changed rapidly in industrial firms in the United States in recent years, and new or modified procedures can be expected in the future as better ways to manage are sought. The nature and time pattern of the evolutionary steps in planning systems have varied between specific companies, but the changes in the International Business Machines Corporation (IBM) illustrate the changes which have taken place to varying degrees in many other companies. Therefore, the major planning developments in IBM up to 1967, as described by the Corporate Planning Department, are reviewed in order of their occurrence.

1. In pre-World War II days, planning was informal and was tied in with operating needs, such as inventory, production, and financing.
2. After World War II, as the company's product line, its sales, and its investment needs expanded, and as technological changes became more frequent, financial planning and product planning were set up as separate entities.
3. During the 1950's, these same changes accelerated. As a result, planning became a part of each functional area—Marketing, Manufacturing, Service, Personnel, etc.—and more concerned with the longer view.
4. Toward the end of the 1950's, the need for integrating and enlarging these planning efforts became apparent. A formal strategic (long range) planning organization was created and procedures requiring all divisions and subsidiaries to prepare annually strategic and operating plans were instituted in 1959. The strategic plans covered five years, while the operating plans were for the current two years.
5. Beginning in 1961, each division initiated an effort to systematize its planning procedures for computer operations. By 1965, most divisions had put together various computer programs for planning data recording, including dynamic models of certain business functions, to assist in the evaluation of alternative courses of action.
6. In 1966, this divisional planning process was extended to seven years with virtually continuous updating of the summary and back-up data on computer and an official annual review. In addition to this change to continuous divisional seven-year planning, a corporate strategic plan was formalized to provide guidance to divisional planning by establishing a limited number of key objectives for each division and subsidiary.
7. Since 1966, increased management attention has been given to planning procedures, and a company wide effort to develop an internally consistent and compatible network of planning data systems was initiated.

Among the 45 companies which were investigated, some could be classified in almost any one of the planning stages mentioned. However, only about 15 of them were still in stages 1, 2, and 3 as of 1965. The movement toward more formal planning systems has been very rapid in the 1960's, for at least 11 of these 45 companies made major organizational changes in 1964 or late in 1963 which introduced formal long-range planning. Others elected new planning officers in 1965, and several of the companies have been engaged in formalized planning activities for only a few years. Of these 45 major corporations, 38 had formalized long-range planning to some extent as of 1965, and most of this group had reached stage 4 or higher in the pattern of evolution previously outlined.

One Vice President reported that long-range planning activities in his company would be more formalized in about two years, and he added that "a concept of how the company ought to be organized for maximum effectiveness has been evolving for five years." The Manager of Personnel and Training in another company which had not formalized planning stated:

> I would predict that within the next five years, our methods of long-range planning will become more sophisticated and more precise; we are obviously moving in this direction, but we still have a long way to go.

The evolution toward formal planning took place in business firms as existing functions were shifted or combined or as new departments were formed for specialized functions such as product development, acquisitions, market planning, or corporate planning. One group often got involved in a wider and wider scope of activities, and when the need for formalized planning became evident and the necessary leadership existed, this group became the nucleus for a formal planning function.

In other instances, an experienced individual from within the company, or at times from an external source, was designated as the Director of Planning in an effort to give more attention to this important function. In some companies, a management consulting firm recommended this action.

Often a Vice President was assigned certain planning responsibilities, as in nearly half of the companies which were studied. The Controller was elected to the position of Vice President—Planning—early in 1965 in one company which started the nucleus of its present planning department in the late 1940's to make economic analyses. Thus, long range planning systems usually evolved slowly, but the common pattern since World War II has been toward more formalized corporate planning.

PITFALLS IN FORMAL LONG-RANGE PLANNING SYSTEMS

Some formal planning organizations failed when they were first introduced. The type of organization which was most likely to become ineffective was one which included only a long-range planning committee, but no full-time staff planners. On the other hand, a corporate planning staff which assumed a centralized, paternalistic planning role was sometimes short-lived.

One company which established a planning function only at the corporate level initially found that operating managers resented the activities of corporate planners and considered them intruders. However, after divisional planning functions were established in this company, cooperation was improved greatly.

Another company abandoned a formal corporate planning function in 1964, but some divisions in the firm retained formal planning assignments. The corporate planning function was apparently eliminated when the company adopted a "group management" philosophy which emphasized committee decisions and a high degree of decentralization. However, the systematic procedures for planning which were developed by the corporate planning staff were still being used in 1966, according to the former Director of Planning at the corporate level.

These incidents indicate that a decision to formalize long-range planning does not insure satisfactory results. However, if a sound philosophy of management is adopted, if planning assignments are clearly defined to both staff planners and line managers, and if competent, cooperative personnel can be found, the probability of success with formalized planning becomes much higher.

CURRENT TRENDS IN FORMALIZED PLANNING SYSTEMS

Several significant trends in corporate long-range planning were indicated by the discussions and correspondence with executives and planners in major business firms.

First, there was a shift away from functional planning and traditional capital budgeting to broader business planning which pertained to products, markets, profits, investments, etc. over extended time periods. However, the allocation of limited funds among competing alternative uses was still one of the major functions in formal planning systems.

Another trend which paralleled the broadening of the scope of long-range planning was the emphasis on planning for the corporation as a whole and not merely for divisions or subsidiaries of the firm. There was much more integration of planning for all units, and what was best for one unit was not necessarily best for the entire company. Therefore, divisions were generally not as independent as in the past when divisionalization and decentralization of authority were carried to great lengths. In many firms, each division was required to use consistent planning formats and financial schedules so that divisional plans could be consolidated into a corporation plan which indicated the expected financial performance of the firm in future years. This requirement also permitted more valid comparisons of divisional plans and more consistent evaluations of subsequent performance.

CHANGES IN PLANNING PROCEDURES

The planning procedures in many firms were being formalized to a greater extent than in previous years. By this action, the assignments of planning responsibilities were clearer and the channels of information flow were more specific. Also, the timing and sequence of planning activities were more rigid, and the procedures for reviewing, approving, and implementing plans were more consistent and more clearly outlined. The experience of many planning coordinators indicated that procedures, assignments, and schedules had to be written out if formal plans were to be reasonably uniform and available at a given time. However, these instructions needed to be relatively simple to gain acceptance from operating managers and to reduce the preparation time for specific plans.

Therefore, in spite of an increase in formal (written) planning instructions, many firms were seeking ways to simplify their long-range plans so that only the most vital information was required. Thus, the planning instructions were becoming less complex, and strict accounting rules were being relaxed.

As part of this trend to maximize the benefit from each expenditure of planning effort, several companies had reduced the future time span for which financial projections and plans were made. Also, the amount of detail which was required had been reduced sharply. Their experience had indicated that projections for many sub-categories of sales and expenses for four or five years into the future became obsolete very rapidly. A notable exception to this trend toward shorter-term planning was the change in IBM in 1966 from five-year to seven-year strategic planning.

Planning for the short term and the long term was more closely related than in previous years, and this apparently was a very recent development. Budgets generally grew out of the broader, long-range plans and corresponded to the financial data in them. Plans for the coming year were typically an integral part of a company's long-range plan.

Operations research techniques and electronic computers were being utilized for a wide range of applications in long-range planning. Specific uses included: economic and demand forecasting; facility planning and plant location; profitability analysis of alternative production, transportation, and marketing plans; and analysis of alternative investment opportunities. At least one company was trying to develop a simulation model which would include all major variables that influenced the performance of the entire firm. The most recent developments in IBM, as outlined in a preceding section, reflect the increasing utilization of computers for planning. As computer systems and analytical techniques are refined, they may revolutionize operational planning and long-range strategic planning in business firms in the next few years.

Planning for the future was a more continuous activity in most firms than in previous years. This development seemed to reflect the increasing formalization and the dynamic nature of planning. Long-range plans were not finalized in discreet, sequential steps, as commonly portrayed in the management literature. Instead, there was a continual interplay and feedback between the major steps of planning, execution, and control. These steps included environmental analysis, objective-setting, strategy-formulation, programming, plan implementation, and performance evaluation. A change in the input variables which were pertinent to any one of these steps often required a revision in specific elements of one or more of the other steps.

A final trend was the effort by some firms to formulate and write down meaningful corporate objectives. This action was considered necessary in order to provide a better foundation for long-range planning. Many of the existing creed-type objectives were of little value as bases for concrete planning.

EXPANDING ROLE OF STAFF PLANNING SPECIALISTS

In the companies which had formalized long-range planning, permanent planning specialists were assigned to the staff at corporation headquarters, and many operating divisions also had full- or part-time planning staffs. These staff planners had important roles to fulfill in the process of corporate long-range planning. The scope of their activities was apparently becoming broader and the extent of their influence was becoming greater.

Corporate planning staffs performed many different functions. They developed planning instructions and schedules, advised operating managers who developed plans, coordinated planning activities, reviewed plans, and proposed revisions or extensions of plans. They also evaluated new business ventures in some firms, and sought new investment opportunities which extended beyond existing divisional activities.

In some companies, a single director of corporate planning performed these functions, while in others, a group of specialists ranging up to 80 or more in number served in this capacity. In a few corporations, the controller's staff coordinated planning activities, but their efforts were directed mostly toward the financial aspects of future activities.

Divisional planning staffs served primarily as coordinators of all planning activities in their respective units. However, in some companies, they performed many of the same functions as corporate planners, but their functions were usually more narrow in scope.

The functional role and degree of participation in long-range planning by staff groups varied widely between companies. Specialized service staffs performed business and market research, economic and demand forecasting, financial analysis, and product planning in most of the companies, whether a formal staff planning function existed or not. Only one of the corporations which was investigated had grouped all of these specialized staffs with planning-related responsibilities into a single planning and development division.

In a few companies, the role of corporate planning staffs was to develop plans and not merely to coordinate the planning efforts by operating managers. This situation was especially evident in two major steel corporations.

Thus, staff planners were an integral part of every formalized long-range planning system, and their role was generally a coordinating one. The position of "corporate staff planning coordinator" is considered essential in any formal planning system. The person who fills this assignment should have an intimate knowledge of the business and a close working relationship with the operating managers.

A corporate planning staff is likely to be most effective if it is located apart from the controller's staff in the organization structure. Also, the size of such a staff should be restricted so that the benefits derived justify the cost. The responsibilities of staff planners should be clearly defined so that such persons serve to complement the efforts of operating managers instead of competing with them in a harmful way.

Planning Responsibility of Operating Managers

In a large majority of the companies, long-range planning was viewed as the primary responsibility of operating managers at various levels in the organization. This was especially true for operational planning of existing activities, and some division heads actively sought new ventures. However, the nature, extent, and degree of long-range planning activities varied considerably between the divisions of various companies and even between the divisions of a particular company.

This variability in planning activities reflected wide differences in the interest, efforts, or capabilities of the operating managers who were responsible for planning. As a result, the value to a firm of the plans which were developed ranged from very high to very low.

The process of developing an awareness of the need and importance of long-range planning in operating managers was apparently a very slow and difficult task. Planning specialists and executives in some companies believed that a period of three to five years was necessary to improve the planning effectiveness of managers to the point where the formal long-range planning system worked properly.

The task of educating managers was usually done by the corporate planning director or by top executives who could visualize the needs and problems in long-range planning. Internal training programs can also be utilized to help managers plan more effectively, and business schools can offer more broad, integrating courses to help future business managers recognize the vital role of planning.

Some companies were making deliberate efforts to get managers to think in broader terms—to take the corporate view. These managers were encouraged to consider longer periods of time and to make more careful plans to support their forecasts. Of course, many operating managers prepared well-developed long-range plans, and in some companies, good plans from one division were used as examples for other divisions to follow.

Thus, operating managers generally had a major responsibility for planning short-range and long-range activities. The function of planning, along with organizing, directing, and controlling, was considered an integral part of every managers job.

SUMMARY APPRAISAL OF FORMALIZED LONG-RANGE PLANNING

In industrial corporations, as in other business firms, planning the type of activities to be pursued in future years is an important function of the managers of each enterprise. If this task is neglected, profitable opportunities may be lost, necessary resources may not be available when needed, and operations can become very inefficient.

In recent years, the planning function of business managers has become more complex and even more essential. Technology has advanced very rapidly, company assets have multiplied, markets have expanded across the world, required investment levels have increased, and the external environment has been in a constant state of flux due to social, political, and economic changes.

In order to cope with the vast number of complex problems and future-related decisions, some companies have formalized the function of long-range planning to various degrees. This action has resulted in more clearly-defined assignments of planning responsibilities, more systematic planning procedures, written instructions and timetables for preparing business plans, standardized formats for financial projections, and a clear-cut procedure for the review and approval of plans. In this way, managers have sought to prepare for expanding activities, to improve operating efficiency, to find profitable new business opportunities, and to avoid pitfalls in the ever-changing business environment.

Among the 45 companies which were investigated, most of them had formalized long-range planning to some extent, and over half of them had assigned important planning functions to a staff officer. Many of these firms were enthusiastic about formalized long-range planning and believed that several significant benefits had been derived from their formal planning systems. Increased profits was the all-encompassing result which was usually attributed to formal planning. Other results which were beneficial included more rapid changes in "direction," sounder investment decisions, and more efficient integration of all corporation activities.

Some problems were also evident in formal planning systems. In some companies, the top executives or operating managers gave an inadequate amount of time and effort to planning activities. Other problems resulted from conflicts between line and staff personnel, unrealistic financial projections, inefficient committee action, and frequent losses of planning specialists to operating positions. However, the realized and potential benefits of formal planning were much greater in magnitude than these problems.

Long-range planning effectiveness in each firm seemed to depend more on the action of the company's President than on any other single factor. Many Presidents endorsed and supported planning activities through approvals, announcements, and requests. However, in the firms which had the most dynamic planning systems, the President also demonstrated his interest and belief in the importance of planning by active discussion of planning procedures, proposed plans, and the results of approved and implemented plans. He evaluated plans carefully before they were approved and also reviewed performance just as carefully to insure that goals were achieved. Thus, a dynamic President who made planning an integral part of his management philosophy was most likely to obtain effective planning efforts from his subordinates.

I believe firmly that every business corporation should have a formal long-range planning system in order to force managers to formulate specific goals and to develop concrete plans for achieving them. However, such a system does not need to be complex. A planning coordinator should be designated, standardized procedures and a planning timetable should be specified in a simple planning guide, and written long-range plans should be developed in each operating unit. A consolidated plan should be prepared by combining unit plans and incorporating new business ventures. The time span should be at least three years, and for certain types of activity, plans and projections for a longer period may be needed.

This type of planning system is most desirable because it permits a firm to realize the major benefits of both divisional and centralized planning. It could be called an integrated "bottom-up" and "top-down" system, and was the typical one which had evolved in the companies with a few years of formalized planning experience.

In this approach, division managers have an opportunity to develop their own plans within broad corporation policy limits on expected earnings, rates of return on investments, and types of business activities. These plans are then integrated into a corporation plan, conflicts or inconsistencies are resolved, and the available capital is allocated to those proposals which are considered best for the corporation. In addition, corporate staff specialists seek new ventures, strategies, or innovations which extend beyond current divisional activities.

An essential part of developing such a system is to develop good managers—those that understand both corporate and unit goals and the complex interactions of the external, internal, and competitive environments. By providing a systematic method of planning, individual managers at all levels in a firm will be able to perform more effectively and more efficiently in providing goods and services to society, while earning a satisfactory level of corporation profits for an indefinite period of time.

Bibliography

Allis-Chalmers Annual Report—1964 (West Allis, Wis.: Allis-Chalmers Manufacturing Company, 1965).

American Management Association, *New Products—New Profits* (New York: American Management Association, Inc., 1964).

Ansoff, H. Igor, *Corporate Strategy: An Analytic Approach to Business Policy for Growth and Expansion* (New York: McGraw-Hill Book Company, Inc., 1965).

Branch, Melville C., *The Corporate Planning Process* (New York: American Management Association, Inc., 1962).

Bright, James R., *Research, Development, and Technological Innovation* (Homewood, Ill.: Richard D. Irwin, Inc., 1964).

Bright, James R. (ed.), *Technological Planning on The Corporate Level* (Boston: Harvard University, 1962).

Chamberlain, Neil W., *The Firm: Micro-Economic Planning and Action* (New York: McGraw-Hill Book Company, Inc., 1962).

Clamp, J. C., "The 'Total' Concept of Company Growth Planning," *Industrial Development and Manufacturers Record,* CXXXII, No. 9 (September, 1963), 14–16.

Corplan Associates, *Technological Change—Its Impact on Industry in Metropolitan Chicago.* Vol. VII: *Industries of the Future;* Vol. VIII: *Summary of: Need, Opportunity and Recommended Action* (Chicago: Corplan Associates, 1964).

Drucker, Peter F., *Managing For Results—Economic Tasks and Risk-Taking Decisions* (New York: Harper & Row, Publishers, 1964).

Ewing, David W. (ed.), *Long-Range Planning for Management* (2d ed. revised; New York: Harper & Row, Publishers, 1964).

"Focusing Farther and Sharper: Stanford Research Institute Has Developed Ways to Organize Long-Range Planning," *Business Week,* No. 1761 (June 1, 1963), 54–61.

Gass, Saul I., *Linear Programming Methods and Applications* (2d ed. revised; New York: McGraw-Hill Book Company, Inc., 1964).

General Motors Annual Report—1964 (New York: General Motors Corporation, 1965).

Gilmore, F. F., and R. G. Brandenburg, "Anatomy of Corporate Planning," *Harvard Business Review,* XL, No. 6 (November–December, 1962), 61–69.

Granger, Charles H., "The Hierarchy of Objectives," *Harvard Business Review,* XLII, No. 3 (May–June, 1964), 63–74.

Hill, William E. "Planning for Profits: A Four-Stage Method," *California Management Review,* I, No. 3 (Spring, 1959), 28–38.

"Into the Big Time," *Forbes,* XCV, No. 4 (February 15, 1965), 29.

Jerome, William Travers III, *Executive Control—The Catalyst* (New York: John Wiley & Sons, Inc., 1961).

Johnson, Richard A., Fremont E. Kast, and James E. Rosenzweig, *The Theory and Management of Systems* (New York: McGraw-Hill Book Company, Inc., 1963).

Le Breton, Preston P., and Dale A. Henning, *Planning Theory* (Englewood Cliffs, N. J.: Prentice-Hall, Inc., 1961).

Leontief, Wassily W., "The Structure of the U. S. Economy," *Scientific American,* CCXII, No. 4 (April, 1965), 25–35.

Lovewell, Paul J., and Robert B. Young, "The Importance of Environment in Company Growth," *A Management Sourcebook,* ed. Franklin G. Moore (New York: Harper & Row, Publishers, 1964), pp. 2–8.

Mace, Myles L., "The President and Corporate Planning," *Harvard Business Review,* XLIII, No. 1 (January–February, 1965), 49–62.

May, William F., "Effective Management—Meeting the Challenge of Change." An Address before the Thirty-third National Packaging Conference, New York, N. Y., April 20, 1964.

National Association of Accountants, *Long-Range Profit Planning,* Research Report No. 42 (New York: National Association of Accountants, December, 1964).

1964 Annual Report—General Electric (New York: General Electric Company, 1965).

Orcutt, Guy H., "Microanalytic Models of Socioeconomic Systems: A New Approach to Forecasting," *Papers Presented to the Ninth Annual Conference on the Economic Outlook at The University of Michigan* (Ann Arbor: The University of Michigan, 1961).

Orcutt, Guy H., Martin Greenberger, John Korbel, and Alice M. Rivlin, *Microanalysis of Socioeconomic Systems: A Simulation Study* (New York: Harper & Brothers, Publishers, 1961).

Payne, Bruce, *Planning for Company Growth* (New York: McGraw-Hill Book Company, Inc., 1963).

Pryor, Millard H., Jr., "Planning in a Worldwide Business," *Harvard Business Review,* XLIII, No. 1 (January–February, 1965), 130–139.

Rapoport, Leo A., and William P. Drews, "Mathematical Approach to Long Range Planning," *Harvard Business Review,* XL, No. 3 (May–June, 1962), 75–87.

Ruzic, Neil P., "The Case for Technological Transfer," Part VII of "The Case for Going to the Moon," *Industrial Research,* VII, No. 3 (March, 1965), 67–87.

Schumpeter, Joseph A., *Capitalism, Socialism, and Democracy* (3d ed.; New York: Harper & Brothers, Publishers, 1950).

Scott, Brian W., *Long-Range Planning in American Industry* (New York: American Management Association, Inc., 1965).

Smalter, Donald J., "The Influence of Department of Defense Practices on Corporate Planning," *Proceedings of the Seventh Annual Symposium on Planning,* ed. E. Kirby Warren (Pleasantville, N. Y.: The Institute of Management Sciences, 1965), pp. 37–60.

Smalter, Donald J., and Rudy L. Ruggles, Jr., "Six Business Lessons From the Pentagon," *Harvard Business Review,* XLIV, No. 2 (March–April, 1966), 64–75.

Stanton, Ted, *The Wall Street Journal,* June 25, 1964, p. 10.

Steiner, George A. (ed.), *Managerial Long-Range Planning* (New York: McGraw-Hill Book Company, Inc., 1963).

"There's A New Tune at Motorola," *Business Week,* No. 1912 (April 23, 1966), 111–114.

Thompson, Stewart, *How Companies Plan,* AMA Research Study No. 54 (New York: American Management Association, Inc., 1962).

Tilles, Seymour, "How to Evaluate Corporate Strategy," *Harvard Business Review,* XLI, No. 4 (July–August, 1963), 111–121.

Tilles, Seymour, *Strategic Planning in the Multi-Divisional Company* (Boston: Boston Safe Deposit and Trust Company, The Management Consulting Division, November, 1964).

Tomb, John O., "A New Way to Manage—Integrated Planning and Control," *California Management Review,* V, No. 1 (Fall, 1962), 57–62.

Warren, E. Kirby, *Long-Range Planning: The Executive Viewpoint* (Englewood Cliffs, N. J.: Prentice-Hall, Inc., 1966).

Weinberg, Robert S., "A Corporate Model as a Tool for Long-Range Planning." Unpublished proceedings of the Eighth Annual Symposium on Planning, April 26 and 27, 1965, New York, N. Y. Sponsored by The Institute of Management Sciences, College on Planning.

Weingartner, H. Martin, *Mathematical Programming and the Analysis of Capital Budgeting Problems* (Englewood Cliffs, N. J.: Prentice-Hall, Inc., 1963).

Whalen, Richard C., "I.M.C.: The Miner Who Shook the Fertilizer Market," *Fortune,* LXXI, No. 3 (March, 1965), 108–113ff.

Index